Model BEHAVIOR
Get *coached* · Get *booked* · Get *paid*

THEE DANIELLE BAKER

Copyright © 2017 by Danielle M. Jones | ISBN: 978-0-9988604-0-4

All rights reserved. No portion of this book or parts thereof may not be reproduced in any form, stored in any retrieval system, or transmitted in any form by any means—electronic, mechanical, photocopy, recording, scanning, or other—except quotations in critical reviews or articles, without prior written permission of the publisher.

Please do not participate in or encourage the piracy of copyrighted materials in violation of the author's rights. If you would like to share this book with another person, please purchase an additional copy for each recipient. If you're reading this book and did not purchase it, or it was not purchased for your use only, then please purchase your own copy. Thank you for respecting the hard work of this author.

Although the author and have made every effort to ensure that the information in this book was correct at press time, the author do not assume and hereby disclaim any liability to any party for any loss, damage, or disruption caused by errors or omissions, whether such errors or omissions result from negligence, accident, or any other cause. The author also cannot warranty or guarantee success. The advice of the author is based on personal experiences, opinion for informational purposes only and do not represent the opinions of any third party.

Cover Art, Format & Design: Lori Kirkpatrick

Ordering Information:
Quantity sales. Special discounts are available on quantity purchases by corporations, associations, and others. For details, contact www.modelbehavior.life

MODEL BEHAVIOR: **GET COACHED.** GET BOOKED. GET PAID.

FOREWORD

Influencer. Visionary. Leader. Creator. No one word encompasses this creative genius. I couldn't imagine the impact of how meeting this woman would enhance my fashion career, brand, and family. Our first meeting was for me to photograph Danielle and her team of models. I was then a practicing photographer taking pictures in my second bedroom. Mrs. Baker-Jones asked, "So, what all is it that you do?" while looking around at a sea of creative mediums, "Whatever needs to be done," I answered. She then responded, "I know, that's right," and I later came to understand she lived by the same motto. She was already a young woman knowing her skills and just needed the time and opportunity to perfect them. That was the first of many "meeting of the minds" conversations we had over the next fifteen-plus years. Over that time, I grew into becoming a fashion designer, celebrity stylist, and boutique owner. Entrusting only her and her team to represent my collection in her shows' nothing short of an "over the top" full fashion production. Soon she exclusively produced all my major shows and fashion events; she ran a tight ship of production, casting, choreography, visuals, and set design—all mastered by her and delegated throughout the team. The first time I watched her work, I was in awe and shocked at all the time I had to concentrate on my designs and visuals, and not the system behind the scenes. From that point on, I have watched as social media, television, and radio boast the achievements, accolades, and empowerment fueled by Mrs. Danielle Baker-Jones, Signature Ink, and Girls GLAM. Throughout the years, I've witnessed that young lady I first met in my apartment studio become a woman, sister to me, mother, wife, and a true Fashion Icon.

Natalie Karyl
Designer, Ragdolls Couture
Owner, The Doll House Boutique

THEE DANIELLE BAKER

ACKNOWLEDGEMENTS

God, my whole heart is filled with thanksgiving from my innermost being. Giving You all the praise and all the honor. Thank You for giving me purpose. Thank You for giving me vision. Thank You for direction, strength, and all of Your countless blessings.

I would like to express my extreme passionate gratitude to my King, my best friend, soul-mate, and true love…my husband Jamarr Jones. You have given me an immeasurable amount of love and support with not only this book but in everything I do. I look forward to continuing spending my life loving you without limits. It's an honor to be your wife and bonus mom to our beautiful girls, Jordan, Jade, and Jewel.

Brasela—Mommy's mini-me. You are my heartbeat; having you gave me more reasons to be all that I can be. Being your first role model, first friend, and first love is a blessing I don't take lightly. When you grow up, strive to be just like you and no one else. Even as your first role model, I want you to be better than me.

Singing Mommaaaaaaa, you know I loveeeee youuuuu! Thank you for always encouraging me and never letting me give up on my dreams and for teaching me how to become a strong woman and work for what I wanted in life. I'm grateful to be able to pass down all you have instilled in me to my girls. Generations to come will be blessed for all of your sacrifices and guidance.

To my Dad and Sister (Alfred and Dana Baker)

I'm missing ya'll like crazy. I know that your loving presence and spirit is with me today and everyday.

My big brothers, well you know who you are. You, too, are like my real life-lifelines. Thank you for being there for me and supporting me always. For walking me down the aisle on my wedding day and for being loving brothers. Your support has added value to my life that I'll never forget.

MODEL BEHAVIOR: **GET COACHED.** GET BOOKED. GET PAID.

Aunt Valerie Dobson—or "Auntie" when I want something…lol. You have held me down since day one with all of my business ventures. Thank you for being my financial advisor for both Signature Ink Modeling Co and Girls GLAM, LLC. You're more than my financial advisor, you're my aunt and my friend. I love and appreciate you even when we fuss about you cutting my budget. Thank you.

Mary Lucas, what would I do if I didn't have you there with all my late nights and early morning deadlines. Every time I needed your expert business advice in a crunch, you produced. Thank you.

Cheryl Smith, from your help with Stare Production to helping me with Model Behavior and all the sisterhood in between, thank you. Terise Smith, thank you for sharing with the world your experience with me as your model coach in a chapter from your first book, "Dream Big & Never Small."

Many thanks, to my backstage manager, Tracy Allen—the organizer. Talk about running a tight ship. You come through for the come through, Honey (flips hair). I appreciate you always having my back through everything.

I'm forever grateful for all of the models that have ever been a part of Signature Ink and Girls GLAM and those who have taken model coaching with me. Thank you for entrusting me and allowing me to make a positive deposit in your journey with memories that will last a lifetime. I wasn't just your coach, agent, or director—you all became family. So much love to you.

Thank you to each and every one of you who has purchased this book. My sincere hope is that you will find invaluable information within its pages.

Contents

I   Foreword

II   Acknowledgements

Get Coached

V   Introduction

1   STAGE 1: Types of Modeling

7   STAGE 2: Self-Esteem Behaviors

15   STAGE 3: My Daily Investment (MDI)

25   STAGE 4: Photo Shoot Ready

37   STAGE 5: Runway Behaviors

49   STAGE 6: Model Coaches, Mentors & Modeling Schools

Get Booked

57   STAGE 7: Agency vs. Freelance Modeling

63   STAGE 8: Casting Behaviors

77   STAGE 9: Benefits of Overcoming Rejection

Get Paid

83   STAGE 10: Image Is Power

103   STAGE 11: You Are The Brand & The Boss

115   STAGE 12: "Show Me The Money"

MODEL BEHAVIOR: **GET COACHED.** GET BOOKED. GET PAID.

INTRODUCTION
Get *coached* · Get *booked* · Get *paid*

You have selected a very exciting field of interest, filled with so many beautiful things. I must say, though, this industry is both "The Beauty and the Beast." Normally before someone gets into the industry, they only see the beauty or they get the chance to experience the beauty side in the beginning. But, trust me, the beast awaits. It's living, breathing, and ready to bite, attack, chew you up, and spit you out at anytime. It hides behind rejection and screams louder than fear. It's the NO you get when you worked so hard to be chosen. It's when a director yells at you, and you feel embarrassed in front of everyone. Or it can be your own voice haunting you when you feel you could have done better. Don't worry—this book will prepare you to be fearless and become the best version of yourself. You'll find that you have to unleash your own beast from time to time. One of the exciting things about Model Behavior is the way you're going to be impacted for modeling, but you'll also be able to apply these principles directly to your life.

I was once the girl who felt like no matter how much I wanted to model, I couldn't because I was too short and curvy for what the modeling industry wanted. Well that's what all the go-sees, designers, and agencies were saying, so it had to be true. Right? WRONG. I learned the benefits of overcoming rejection and how to push through toward my goals. When I did some research, certain information categorized me as a plus-size model, and other information didn't even acknowledge curvy at all. My creative wardrobe didn't make it any better, either; it actually left me feeling like a misfit. I couldn't wrap my mind around all the limitations put on the modeling industry. My mom put me in modeling classes at the age of 6. I loved modeling as a child—traveling, competing in pageants, and walking runways. As I got older, and I wasn't a kid anymore, things really got real for me. My skin wasn't thick enough for all the rejection and mean words. I couldn't wrap my brain around the models that became extremely ill to be the size clients were looking for and that some even developed eating disorders and died.

That may not be your story; maybe you're the industry's height and size but frustrated because you're not getting callbacks to even begin getting paid.

Consider this book priceless! You've made a tiny investment compared to what you will gain by reading this book and applying this information to your life. Don't just read this book, study it, and get fully involved in the model challenges

I will personally share some of my good and ugly experiences in my career. Learn from my mistakes, and grow from what I have gained. This book is to help guide you. What I'm sharing with you did not exist in a step-by-step format when I started out. There weren't a lot of recent data to help me get started or enhance the experiences I already had. I didn't have someone to coach me along the way and answer all the questions I had. And surely no one was even attempting to hire short or curvy girls.

However, the good news is, the modeling industry is changing in a way that is opening up to give more models opportunities outside of tradition. Also, models are becoming their own brand. If I would have given up 15 years ago, I wouldn't have the experience to share with you today. A few celebrity designers personally told me DON'T re-invent the wheel, but I had to for all the models who were experiencing what I was and all those who fit the requirements but were not getting booked—for all the models who did fit the industry requirements, but had no idea how to get started or what they really needed to do to be able do what they loved. The industry didn't have what I needed, so I created my own lane by taking a leap of faith and having the tenacity to start a modeling company that represented models of all shapes, sizes, heights, and cultures. I prayed for a book like this when I was younger to help guide and direct me to Get Coached, Get Booked, & Get Paid. I had no idea that I would become the author to fulfill those needs and bring change.

All aspiring models, paid or trying to get paid, tall or short, thin or curvy can benefit from this book. Know that I have aligned model behavior to work internally first to prepare you for the modeling industry and the betterment of your life. If you desire to be a model, then decide what kind of model you want to be and step into your dream and become one.

Throughout this book, you and I will begin to form a one-on-one relationship. Consider me your model coach. As your coach it is important to get you where you want to be as fast as possible. Applying the principles you learn here can get you closer to living your dreams with your eyes open. Contact me directly for personal model coaching, with and plan designed to accomplish your personal goals. Don't give up; your future needs your help now. It's time to boss up.

MODEL AFFIRMATION

Speak this over your life every morning. Believe it and receive it.

"I AM WORTHY to look good, feel good and to be in love with my life. I know that the effort I put in today will be an investment into my dreams. I show up for myself, my goals and for my brand. Professional clients are attracted to my magnetic personality. *Today I have the ability to Get Coached, Get Booked and Get Paid!*"

MODEL BEHAVIOR: **GET COACHED.** GET BOOKED. GET PAID.

This book is dedicated to you!

Let my many hours of courageous labor, hard lessons learned, sleepless nights, hurt, and sad tears that became tears of joy be to your benefit. I dedicate this book to you.

MODEL BEHAVIOR: **GET COACHED.** GET BOOKED. GET PAID.

STAGE 1
types of modeling

Most people are familiar with Runway Modeling. With the height, weight, and body type standards being so strict, it is very difficult for most men and women to meet the requirements. Believe it or not, some models are rejected for being too tall, or too skinny. Does this mean you will never become a model? Not at all. There are different types of modeling, meaning different divisions in the industry.

There is a list of "20 Types of Modeling," which some you may be familiar with and others may not. First, let's start with what the word "model" really means so you can fully understand your job description. It's always best to get the full meaning of a word before you assume.

A **model** is a person who is serving as a visual guide to promote, display, and or advertise a product or service. Keep this in mind as you view this list.

1. **Commercial Model** The largest division of modeling covering print advertisement, including catalogs, magazines, billboards, and posters, as well as digital ads and TV commercials.

2. **Entertainment Model** Models that mix runway walks with dance movements. They are there to entertain the audience, not to sell clothing.

3. **Fashion/Runway Model** Female height requirements are 5'8–5'11, and male requirements are 5'11–6'2.

4. **Petite Model** Categorized as models who are smaller built.

5. **Plus Model** Models who have larger measurements with defined curves.

6. **Child Model** Typically a child under the age of 12 that is hired to advertise, display, and promote commercial products.

7. **Super Model** High profile, highest paid, national/international ads and celebrity status.

8. **Spokes Model** A model that is stylishly dressed, well spoken, and associated with a brand in advertisement. Used as the face or voice for specific companies.

9. **Pageant Model** Involves a beauty contest where results are based on judging. Models compete against other models in modeling and talent categories for titles and prizes.

10. **Alternative Model** People who aren't your typical commercial model. This division is niche categories for gothic, fetish, tattooed, and punk.

11. **Specialty/Parts Model** Body parts model for hands, arms, feet, nails, etc. The focus is typically only on a specific part of the body. The face may or may not be shown depending on the specific part.

12. **Mature Model** Mainly fashion models over the age of 40, who still models in their golden years.

13. **Fitness Model** Very healthy and toned physique with defined muscle groups.

14. **Vixen Model** A female model that appears in hip-hop oriented music videos and very sexy magazines.
15. **Lingerie/Glamour Model** Model who have the ability to pose seductively. The one and only focus is sexuality.
16. **Swimsuit Model** Models that are in great shape with great bodies.
17. **Promotional/Event Model** The main focus is to drive customers toward a product, service, or brand and to provide information about the product or service they are promoting.
18. **Fit Model** A person clothing manufactures or fashion designers use to check the fit of a garment.
19. **Trade Show Model** Models work a floor space or booth and represent a company to attendees.
20. **Arts Model** Poses for visual arts purposes.
21. **Hobby Model** One who enjoys modeling and has fun participating in modeling assignments yet does not get paid to model.

There are so many ways you can get into modeling. Did you know these particular types of modeling were available? There are actually more than this, but these are the most common. As you went down the list, did you see where you fall at or where you want to be? I want you to be very specific in choosing the type of modeling you're going to do; this will help you Get Coached, Get Booked, & Get Paid.

Select the type of model you are and write it in your Boss Book. Yes, you can select more than one type.

"I CAN" Challenge

You cannot say the word CAN'T. When you say "I can't," then you won't. When you say "I can," then you will. Tell your three closest friends or family that you spend the most time with that you have eliminated the word can't out of your vocabulary and to hold you accountable. If they hear you say I can't, then you need a consequence. Your consequence can be writing an affirmation 50 times "I can and I will _____" (insert whatever you said can't to) or write 50 times "I can do all things through Christ who strengthens me." May look familiar—it's Philippians 4:13. I know it might take you back to being a kid again writing and such, but it will help build your foundation while eliminating "can't" from your vocabulary. I don't care if you're rolling your eyes or sucking your teeth right now. Do this for YOU. It's best to do it the easy way by writing it. If you continue to say I can't, you'll never reach your full potential. Just by taking that "I can't" out of your vocabulary you change your life. If you ever work with me, the consequences get a little painful for both female and male models. That's how much I want you to succeed. I know what making this change did for me, and it will do the same for you.

MODEL BEHAVIOR: **GET COACHED.** GET BOOKED. GET PAID.

Say "I AM_____."

(name your modeling type)

SAY: *"I CAN and I WILL reach my goals and live my dreams with my eyes open."* This is an affirmation.

This is a photo of an eye on a can. This represents "I can." Until you can show me an "I can't" as an illustration, do not tell yourself that anymore.

List your three to five friends or family members in your Boss Book, contact them right away, and ask them to be your accountability partners. If you do end up with a consequence, you have 24 hours to write it and show it to them. For every time you say "I can't," write 50 times your affirmation "I CAN and I WILL reach my goals and live my dreams with my eyes open." Or write the scripture "I can do all things through Christ who strengthens me."

A boss book is a book you're going to keep all of your ideas, notes and things your working on towards your goals. As you work through Model Behavior, you will be working on you at the same time.

STAGE 2
self-esteem behaviors

Self-Esteem Behaviors

Becoming a model is more than what you see on the outside; it starts internally with your self-esteem and self-love. Before you can start modeling or bring change to your career, I really want you to know yourself. Your confidence level will determine how far you go. Many will say they already know themselves really well—until they find themselves contemplating doing things like this.

I thought I knew myself too, until I had to face myself.

What do you see when you look at this picture?

Do you see pain, hurt, and identity issues? Lack of self-love and low self-esteem? You may even see yourself or someone you know and relate to it. Many experience these emotions in the modeling industry and everyday life. You can see a beautiful image of someone and point out all the reasons why that image is gorgeous and then turn around and compare it to yourself and point out all the reasons you think you're not.

Well, I see someone who doesn't understand herself or who she really is. She has beaten herself up so much in the inside with negative comments that she has created a river of insecurities. She's so low in self-esteem that she's willing to harm herself to look like what she feels is beautiful.

That's a bad behavior that needs to be broken forever. You can look at a gorgeous image and admire it as well as look at yourself and admire you, too.

Don't be tormented by your mind. What kinds of thoughts are really going through your mind? "I just want to cut it off." "I'm so fat, nobody will like me." "I'll never be a model." "I can't take this anymore."

Maybe it's not your body that gives you insecurity about yourself; it could be the feeling behind the bag.

Are you wearing a mask because you feel ugly or you want to be someone else? Do you look at other people and other models and wish you looked that way?

Why do you believe you're ugly or why do you believe you're not as pretty as you want to be? Look at yourself.

How much of what you see and believe about yourself is true? How much of it came from others, and you accepted it?

There is a difference between feeling ugly and believing you are ugly.

Don't get me wrong. I do have days where I feel fat, when my clothing is not fitting right or my hair's a mess, making me feel un-pretty; but that is an emotional feeling that comes and goes. I don't believe it, and I'm certainly not embracing it, allowing it to live with me.

For decades, models allowed the anxiety of getting work and the pressure of making it or the stress of succeeding dictate their way of reaching their goal. In everyday life, eating disorders develop as a way to avoid pain. In the modeling industry, it has developed as a way to get a job. Over time, models have died from eating disorders, such as bulimia. I call that "dying to be thin." Someone once said, "I started under-eating, over-exercising, pushing myself too hard, and brutalizing my immune system."

Please know there is a healthier way available. It starts with your self-esteem.

In sociology and psychology, **self-esteem** *reflects a person's overall subjective emotional evaluation of his or her own worth. It is a judgment of oneself as well as an attitude toward the* **self**.

Stop hating your body and your looks, and start loving yourself more. Don't judge yourself and compare yourself to someone else.

Girls don't just wake up and decide to hate their bodies—people teach them to. They're not born believing they're ugly; society changed them. So if people are taught and can be changed toward the negative, we can teach ourselves and change toward the positive. First, make your list of everything, and I mean everything, negative that you feel or believe about yourself.

> Today I feel:
> - ☐ Like I don't fit in
> - ☐ Ugly
> - ☐ Hurt
> - ☐ Too skinny
> - ☐ Overweight
> - ☐ Useless
> - ☐ Worthless

Now, I need you to know and understand we are all "fearfully and wonderfully made" by our Creator. He created us all in a unique way. Back in my younger school days, I called myself a misfit, and still do. In those days people would joke about my high cheekbones or my "chinky" eyes.

My lower extremities were mainly bigger than everyone else's. I was loud and always creating stuff. Some use to say I wore my brothers' hand-me-downs.

Needless to say, now as an adult, I still call myself a misfit for totally different reasons than before. However, I understand more about myself and accept those jokes that once hurt my feelings as compliments. It's part of what differentiates me from others. The physical appearance I was once teased about is my biggest asset. My high cheekbones are part of the diamond face shape that come from my Apache and Cherokee Indian bloodline. Having larger lower extremities is because

I'm pear-shaped. Nowadays people are having surgical procedures on their lower extremities, and I'm walking around natural. Me being loud and creative was always who I was and played a part in becoming who I am today as a multi-passion business owner.

I first had to love and embrace everything about me, no matter what others would say about me. I told myself I was beautiful and, on my good days, gorgeous. I had to check myself and dig deep into who I was and figure out WHY this was so important to me. My self-esteem hit rock bottom with all the rejection and feeling like an unprepared misfit with no one to help give me direction in the industry. Then, after crying and beating myself up time after time because of the limitations the industry put on me, I STOPPED. Then I started standing on, "For I am fearfully and wonderfully made" in Psalms 139:14 began to resonate in me. All of us are created unique and different. I started to stand on that anytime someone would say, "You're not what we're looking for," or "We chose someone else," or "You're too curvy, your cheekbones are too high, your eyes are too 'chinky,'" etc. In my mind, I would recite Psalms 139:14 over and over and over again. Then I realized it wasn't just the industry making me feel like I wasn't good enough, I was making me feel the same way. Sometimes we believe all the negative things people say about us. I began to look at myself for who I was and not who they were limiting me from being. I couldn't let their opinions of me stop my dreams before they had the opportunity to come to pass. I got very focused on becoming successful no matter what. Researching, studying, practicing, and being fully prepared from castings to go-sees to a paycheck. And now I have made this information available to you right here, right now.

Self-esteem comes from you; no one else can give you self-esteem. Others can build your confidence, yes, but not your self-esteem. It has to come from within you, that's why it's called SELF-esteem. Fall in love with yourself and be your own best friend. Your inner beauty can beat your outer beauty any day.

What to do when you feel fat, ugly, or any of these negative things?

Maybe your self-esteem behavior is not this extreme, but it doesn't mean you're not in a constant struggle with it. Your self-esteem will be tested—everyone's is. This list will be here if you need it.

Now, take that list you wrote previous to this one with all the negative things on it and rip it to shreds. Celebrate as you're tearing it up on the way to the trash can or just throw it in the air; walk on it a few times and sweep it up later.

Teach your self-esteem how to behave. Start feeding it now, so when it starts acting up, get yourself in check.

Self-Esteem Challenge

Now it's your turn. Start a new list of positive features and characteristics about yourself. Write down the things you love about yourself. Even the fact that you are alive is worth writing down as a starting point. When you get to at least ten, type it and add a photo of yourself on the same page. Place it somewhere where you can see it often—places like your mirror, near your charger, on your planner or the wallpaper on your phone/electronic device.

MODEL BEHAVIOR: **GET COACHED.** GET BOOKED. GET PAID.

Self-Esteem Checklist

- ☐ Challenge yourself to acknowledge everything you love about yourself (read your list).
- ☐ Look at a photo of yourself when you looked and felt your best.
- ☐ Remember the compliments others have given you (start keeping them in the notes on your phone if needed to keep them close).
- ☐ Do something you enjoy to change your mood.
- ☐ Be grateful for still being alive to see and embrace your inner and outer beauty.
- ☐ Check yourself—change your diet and fitness routine if needed.
- ☐ Give compliments to others.
- ☐ Make a positive goal pertaining to looking and feeling better about yourself.
- ☐ Love yourself, starting with the inner you.
- ☐ STOP COMPLAINING (this one is even worse than saying "I can't").

STAGE 3
my daily investment

What's mind boggling for me is the people who would do any and everything for someone to invest in them, but they don't even invest in themselves. Don't be that person. We can't expect others to do more for us than we are willing to do for ourselves. My daily investment (MDI) is a strong way to start investing in yourself.

How much time are you spending everyday investing in becoming the best model you can be? Everyday you must do something toward your goals. You're going to pay yourself everyday. I already know what you're thinking—how can I pay myself everyday if I'm not even bringing in money from the industry yet? Great question. The answer is payments come in ways other than money. Some days you will pay yourself in money, other days you will pay yourself in attention, pay yourself in love, in positive energy, etc. Below is a list of 12 payments. I encourage you to do at least one a day. Use your MDI jar to keep all your payments in. This will be like your internal bank. Best practice is to empty your jar after 30 days and review how you did. You can grab a jar and dedicate it as the space for accomplishing your daily investments.

- Attention
- Development (model behavior)
- Love
- Inspiration
- Knowledge
- Money
- Motivation
- Net worth
- Positive energy
- Physically
- Spiritually (scriptures & quotes)
- Study

Go over and beyond by creating an MDI Calendar for you like the one here. Commit to at least 20–30 minutes a day. Aren't you worth investing 20–30 minutes a day to change your life? I'll break each of these down, so you will understand them. It gets fun, too. The more you make a daily investment in yourself, the better your opportunities will get and the inner you will grow.

MONTH

Sunday	Monday	Tuesday	Wednesday	Thursday	Friday	Saturday

This list is in alphabetical order; however, you do not have to pay yourself in this order.

Pay yourself Attention

Look in the mirror for five minutes and talk to yourself about yourself. I know, that sounds crazy right? But do it; it's you against you. Here is where your development starts. Make sure your surroundings are very quiet so that you can hear yourself and your thoughts. Sometimes you may mug or laugh at yourself. Some of us love the mirror, so you will be very open to looking yourself in the mirror for five minutes. Here is exactly what I want you to do:

- Stand in front of the mirror or use a handheld mirror so that you can see your entire face.
- Choose a quiet area so that you can hear yourself and your thoughts.
- Set your alarm or timer for five minutes.
- Use your voice memo on your phone to record your voice.
- Once your timer starts, begin talking to yourself about yourself. Don't bring up other people. Ask yourself "Who am I?" and "What kind of modeling career you I to have?"
- When you ask yourself who you are, include your character, what makes you unique, your best physical features, things that you love, and things that you love to do.

Pay yourself Development

Practice leads to development and confidence. Practice your craft so you can strengthen your craft. Even if you're just starting out, your passion will drive you to want to fully develop yourself. Read, study, and practice what's in this book—it's part of development.

Pay yourself Love

Meaning give yourself an intense feeling of deep affection. Of course, you can do this by telling yourself I love you, but you must feel it, too. One way you can feel it is by writing a love letter to yourself. Don't knock it until you try it.

Outside of that, figure out what you love. One of my favorite authors, Rhonda Byrne, said to list everything you love one by one. Places you love, things you love, people you love, music you love, etc. This was incredibly effective for me, because it really helped me figure out what I loved and to focus more of my attention on it. Once I did that, I begin to attract more of what I loved instead of what I didn't love.

Pay yourself Inspiration/Quotes
Read something or listen to something for 20 minutes in the morning or 20 minutes before you go to bed. Learn quotes from people who inspire you.

Pay yourself Knowledge
Feed your brain with information all the time, and keep yourself in a position to learn. Research specific areas that will help you gain knowledge to enhance your skill. Study, study, study the information you want to retain and get full understanding. Don't be the person who thinks they know it all. As long as you're living, you should be learning.

Pay yourself Money
Yes, you can pay yourself money. A dollar a day at that! There are so many ways you can do this. One could be from the model challenges you complete in this book. Or goals you set for yourself and/or your income (see example under positive energy). You can take it a step further and pay yourself from your income. You'll learn more about this when we get into branding in later chapters. Feel free to increase or decrease the amount you want.

Pay yourself Motivation
Motivation is something that comes from within. We get motivated when we hear motivational speakers and music that encourages our spirit. It's up to us to keep ourselves motivated. We stay motivated by focusing on what we love.

Pay yourself Net worth
Get out and network with other like-minded people and build relationships. Take time and really see who your resources are and connect with them. There is a famous quote that still stands truth today: "Your Network Is Your Net Worth."

Pay yourself Positive energy

Again, yes, you can pay yourself money. I started paying myself a dollar a day for every day I went without negativity. It was hard to do for a year straight, but I did it. No, I didn't end up with $365 at the end of the year, but I did have $287, and now I live a way more positive life. You can challenge yourself to do the same thing or something similar.

Pay yourself Physically

Your health is what keeps you alive. What can you do today to help your future self? Eat clean, exercise, workout. Eliminate stress by getting rid of everything you can control. Even if you have a small build, you can still have your body conditioned.

Pay yourself Spiritually

Take some quiet time every day to pray, read, and study the Word. Meditate and relax your mind to receive direction and answers to all that you're praying for.

The My Daily Investment stage is created for you to build internally. It's also here for you to get to know yourself better and grow.

Got Dreams? Ready, Set, DREAM

What are you daydreaming about?

Daydreaming is a short-term detachment from one's immediate surroundings, during which a person's contact with reality is blurred and partially substituted by a visionary fantasy, especially one of happy, pleasant thoughts, hopes, or ambitions, imagined as coming to pass and experienced while awake.

Some of us haven't had a daydream in years, because of how busy our minds are on distractions or stress, preventing us from drifting off into an ambitious visionary fantasy.

Let's help ourselves live our dreams by focusing on our goals. Setting goals for ourselves and accomplishing them is extremely healthy for our internal being. Take a moment and dig deep into what you really want to accomplish in your life. It's okay if you haven't set goals—now is the time to do so and/or update the ones you have.

Goal Digger
Write down specifically what you want. Believe it or not, some of us get stuck right here. We either don't know what we want, or we aren't specific enough about what we want. This is supposed to be the easy part. Don't keep it in your mind—write it down and make it plain. Be specific when doing this. For example, I want an apple. Being specific would be I want a green apple or I want a red apple. More examples:

Goal	Goal Digger (Be specific)
I want to be in a magazine. →	I want to be in Vogue Magazine.
I want to get paid work. →	Name clients you want to work for.
I want my own place. →	List the number of bedrooms, neighborhood, etc.

Dream Chaser

After you are done making your list of everything you want and turning them into specific goals, you will move into the next stage to chase your dreams. You must know what you're chasing specifically, and it has to be realistic and believable to you. It doesn't matter what other people think, but it totally matters what you think and believe. Activate your chase with a time-sensitive completion date, and stick to it. Some goals may take weeks, a month, or even years—and that's okay. Each goal will need some action steps that lead up to your completion date. Once you have put your completion dates on your goals, your chase can officially begin.

Dream Catcher

Here is where I want you to catch your dreams through visualization. Take your goals and start daydreaming. Get lost in the visualization of what you would love to have in your life. Imagine it as if it has already happened. Gather photos to help put you in that mindset. Create your vision board or update the one you have by gathering specific photos that support each one of your goals. This will put you in the mindset of attracting it. I have multiple vision boards for different areas of my life, but I started out with just one corkboard.

When a goal starts coming to pass, I take it off the front of the board and put it on the back of the board for later encouragement. Every time I need to be encouraged, I look at the back of the board with all the things that have already come to pass. It gives me hope that the things on the front of the board will happen without a doubt. Put your board somewhere that you can see it every day, and give yourself 10–15 minutes to daydream. You can do this along with MDI or separately. Also, feel free to create a digital vision board that you can keep on your phone or computer.

Be extremely specific with the photos you select—it makes all of the difference. For example, if you want to be signed with an agency, which agency? If you want to be in magazines or commercials, which ones? If you want a house, how many bedrooms and what exactly does it have in it? If you want a car, what type of car, what color? Etc. More details on how to use your vision board is in the branding stage of this book under *Set Goals and Activate Them*.

Visions can be displayed on corkboard, a photo frame, post-it, a notebook, or a wall. It's totally up to you.

Dream Thieves

OUCH, this hurts.

Dream thieves are alive and well; don't be naïve. Protect your DREAMS!

The obvious dream thief is one who you share your dreams with, and they go out and do the same exact thing you were doing or wanted to do.

Another dream thief is the kind who tear down your dreams with words. They say stuff like, "You're never going to be able to do it." "That's not going to happen for you." "Get your head out of the clouds" or "You're living in la la land." "That's a crazy idea; you're crazy." "You're stupid for that one." "Look at yourself—do you really think you got a chance? That's not even realistic."

If you're experiencing any of this, get those people away from you if you can. Sometimes it can be your family members, who are always around. But that doesn't mean you have to share your dreams with them.

Truth be told, sometimes you yourself put your dreams down. You allow the words of others to turn into verbal abuse, sabotaging your dreams. They begin to make you feel crazy, and then you let your own dreams start slipping further and further away. It is enough keeping your own thoughts in line with your dreams so that you don't talk yourself out of them. You don't need others around you speaking against your heart's desires.

Dead Dreams

These are the dreams that die inside of people who never gave life to them before they physically passed away. I don't know about you, but I want to go to my grave empty. Every dream inside of me is getting birthed before it's my time to go. Understand that we are all here to serve a purpose. What if Martin Luther King Jr. had never gone after his dream; could you even imagine where the world would be right now?

Dream Living

Take the leap of faith, and make your dreams a reality. Set your goals and believe in them. Live your dreams with your eyes open. Step by step, day by day.

You can do this!!

MODEL BEHAVIOR: **GET COACHED.** GET BOOKED. GET PAID.

STAGE 4
photoshoot-ready

STRIKE A POSE and then pose, pose, pose, pose some more. Keep posing all day, any and everywhere. Try poses that you are uncomfortable holding. Use anything that gives you a reflection of yourself so you can see how you're doing. For example, your shadow, reflection on shining things, etc. This helps out a lot when you're not near a mirror. Another thing you can do is mimic posing. Grab some really good poses from out of a magazine or online and try doing that exact pose. It could help get you comfortable posing until you're able to flow into your own. For stretch and flexibility to create and hold unique poses, try yoga. Some of the most beautiful poses feel awkward and uncomfortable to models, but the shots are electrifying. Models get caught up on getting booked but then struggle with executing in front of the camera. The only way you can get better posing is actually practicing and then evaluating with constructive criticism to get better.

Start with a posing warm up using the poses below. Shake your body out, stretch a little, and get loose. Clear your mind, and tell yourself to pose. Yes, tell yourself what to do. I suggest using a full-length body mirror while practicing. If you don't have a full-length mirror, use the video option on your phone. Begin your posing warm up doing the poses. Hold each pose for at least 60 seconds before going to the next one. This will give you 15 minutes a day of posing warm ups.

After two weeks, you can begin to substitute these poses for the poses you will mimic from top models in the industry. Mimic top models for two weeks as well. That would put you at 30 days, 15 minutes a day doing posing warm ups. As you're doing this, you'll be training your body for posing, and you will be training your mind to focus on it. As time progresses, I want you to come up with your own poses and begin posing without any instruction. You can use the poses you've been practicing as reference points, but do not have them programed in your mind that they are all you do or all you know.

There is an art to posing using all levels of creative activity—connecting the dots between your inner beauty, your outer beauty, your creativity, and your emotional power. It's a place where you can be free; don't think about body moment. JUST POSE.

Here's how…

Flexibility
The more flexible you are, the more unique poses you will be able to do. Stretching often and/or yoga will increase your flexibility.

Arches
Arch your back and side to insinuate body shape.

Hips
Positing your hips creates femininity.

Profile views
Slightly moving your head can bring angles.

Elongate
Always keep your posing in a way that your body appears long. Don't squeeze shoulders or neck. Be cautious of a slight bend of the knees that makes you look shorter.

Unlimited poses
There is such a thing; I teach it all the time. My secret to unlimited posing is restrictions. As you're posing, take a position and hold parts of your body so it cannot move until you run out of posing with the part of the body you can move. Here is an example. Let's say your hands are on your hips and you restrict the top half of your body. Then all you can move is the bottom half of your body… hips, legs, knees, toes. Do all the poses you can do from the waist down. Then choose a pose for the bottom half of your body, restrict it, and then do all the poses with the top half of your body. Trust me, you will do poses you would have never have come up with without restricting. You can restrict your angles, too. Try it.

Try poses that make your body hurt, seriously. Lean to the side until you're about to hit the floor and hold it. Face backwards, but bring your upper body around to the front and hold.

I'm a strict coach, but you'll have a little fun while learning. One of my favorite things I teach models to do is "Posing while in the air." It's fun, but it can be hard.

Here you can incorporate everything all at once. Do this for 15–20 minutes, and you're going to feel like you just had a workout.

The point of this is to make you a stronger poser. While you're in the air, arch, flex, elongate, give face, exercise … everything. This will also help you build up your stamina for long hours on set, freezing outside in swimwear or getting hot flashes while in dressed in Avant Garde fashion. Find a jump facility in your area or a trampoline and get started. Thank me later.

5 Key Elements To a Great Shot

As a model, I need you to know and understand the 5 Key Elements to a great shot. Every time you have a great shot, it collectively becomes a great shoot, and that's what we all want!

1. Mentally
2. Eye Emotions
3. Facial Expressions
4. Body Language
5. Overall Presence (in front of the camera)

First and foremost … BE PREPARED

Having these elements on point each frame at each shoot is what clients pay for.

1. Mentally Prepare for your shoot. The more information you know prior the better. So have clear communication with the person booking your shoot. Get your mindset photo shoot ready. Leave all distractions at the door. When your mind is thinking about the argument you just had with someone, or you're focused on what you have to do after the shoot is not going to have you mentally prepared. Be where you are right now—meaning have your whole mind with you the entire time and not scattered in pieces thinking about multiple things. Take a moment to sit down and think through the entire day and how you want it to go. Pack your bag and stay in that mindset. I don't care how comfortable

you are in front of the camera. You still may feel a bit nervous upon arriving for the shoot or during a shoot. Many times it takes some time to warm up. No matter what level you're on experience-wise, doing these key elements will help you have a successful shoot.

2. Eye Emotions will have your photo talking without you saying a word. To do this, you have to be extremely connected to your inner emotions. Make your thoughts and your emotions become one. Practice this with a mirror but with only your eyes visible.

3. MODEL FACE—Facial Expression is in direct support of your eye emotions. Once your thoughts/mindset have become one, it's easy to get your facial expression in agreement. Practice using a handheld mirror different facial expressions. For example, happy, sad, excited, serious, blank stare, etc. Understand that you can't photo-shop personality; you have to bring it.

4. Body Language can be uncomfortable in the modeling world. Some poses call for flexibility or positioning in ways using muscle you've never used before. Again, I suggest yoga for flexibility; this will set you apart from others. Your pose should be so good that if your head were cropped out of the picture, the pose would still be slaying.

5. Overall Presence on camera is everything above mixed with good energy. A photographer will keep shooting when they get lost in your execution of good energy. If it's hard for them to connect with you, it begins to feel like a waste of time. The more you work at this, the better you will be.

Test Shoots

Test shoots serve such a great purpose. They teach new models many lessons and keep experienced models active and relevant. Test shoots are like dress rehearsals for the big act. I never want you to treat it as practice, though. Treat it like you're getting paid to do a job every time. Have the mindset of a working model.

Now you're at the point you are ready for your first shoot or your next shoot. It's time to incorporate everything from this stage. You want to shoot, but you may not have much money. Starting off doing an exchange can be helpful in ways more than financial.

Look for professionals in your area that are looking for models to exchange TFP (time for prints) or looking to build their portfolios. Normally a photographer offers TFP to test new photography equipment. TFPs are produce 50/50 results in some instances. You want the good 50%. What I mean is that just because a photographer agrees to do TFP shoot doesn't mean they're good. It's a 50% risk you take going about it this way. You can also reach out to friends, family or college students majoring in photography. That's a risk too if the quality of work is not up to par.

I caution you to do thorough research or have someone reliable to do it for you. Everyone is not who they say they are. Unfortunately, some models have been taken advantage of by trusting a photographer who was a scam, who only wanted sexual pleasure, or who put models in an unsafe environment. Getting referrals helps, but you still want to check everything out for yourself. Don't be so excited that someone wants to shoot with you that you put that before your life.

Safety Tips

Make the photographer aware in advance that you're bringing someone with you. Don't bring kids—it's unprofessional and distracting unless they're the models. Don't bring people you're in a relationship with if it's going to make you nervous or uncomfortable. Bring someone who is supportive, has really good positive energy, and understands this is work for you. Everyone on your team should know this is work; it's no different than going to work with someone. Sometimes, depending on the job, they may not allow someone in the actual room as the shoot but right outside the door. If you're told no one at all can be in the building … CAUTION.

Whether you're doing a test shoot or actual print work, HANDLE YOUR BUSINESS.

Have clear communication with the person booking your shoot. Cover the bases with location, type of shoot, people involved in the shoot, and responsibilities—and don't forget about the model releases.

Shoot Location

Get the address at least 3–5 days before your shoot. This will allow you to check the distance and plan your travel. Depending on the area and parking, it maybe best to take a bus or train. I suggest you go to the address prior to the shoot if the distance isn't too far. Believe it or not, going ahead of time saves you a lot of time and fear. It will look familiar to you the second time around and give you a sense of security when you know where you're headed. Do this whether the shoot is on location or in studio. No need to go in unless you already scheduled a quick meet and greet. Otherwise, just go by for your own good.

Weather

Check the forecast as soon as you get your date and again the day before. This can affect the actual shoot if outside, and it's also good to know for traveling purposes. You may need to pack additional items because of the weather.

Type of Shoot

This is where your model bag comes into play big time. Inside your model bag you should have all your basics, from the correct undergarments to an entire outfit.

Upon booking your shoot you should understand the nature of the shoot and the details. For example, editorial, headshots, advertisement for a particular brand, etc.

Even if the designer, stylist, or photographer says you don't need to bring anything, bring your model bag anyway.

The Model Bag

On the next page are helpful items that have become necessities for every model. All model bags need to stay prepared at all times. Model bags should be limited to two bags to pack and carry necessities—bags can be condensed after fittings. Gender requirements are specified. Once you pack up your model bag, triple check to make sure you have everything using this list as your checklist.

Females hair should be clean and free of all products if stylists are on site. Males hair should be groomed before arrival. Both, females and males, should not bring real jewelry, wear perfume or cologne.

Also, while on site, models should not be late, always carry him or herself in a professional manner, and most importantly, ask questions if unsure about any processes.

What's in Your Model Bag?

Grooming: Hair, Makeup & Skincare		Shoes	Wardrobe: Black/Nude	Miscellaneous Items
FEMALES				
☐ Edge Control (Product to lay hair down) ☐ Gel ☐ Any other hair products you normally use ☐ Ponytails holders ☐ Scarf ☐ Comb ☐ Brush ☐ Hair pins ☐ Bobby pins ☐ Holding Spray (travel size) ☐ Flat irons/curlers ☐ Oil Sheen (travel size)	Basic makeup kit with: ☐ Eye shadows ☐ Foundation ☐ Concealer ☐ Blush ☐ Liners ☐ Mascara ☐ Bronzer, and ☐ Eyelashes and glue (optional) ☐ Face Mask ☐ Makeup Remover ☐ Toes and fingernails polish (clear or nude) ☐ Moisturizer ☐ Clear deodorant (no flakes)	Depending on the season of the show and designer, shoes may vary from: ☐ Pumps ☐ Open toe ☐ Wedges ☐ Booties ☐ Knee boots ☐ Small selection of flats (you can never go wrong with black, nude or clear)	☐ Fitted pants ☐ Top/cami ☐ Dress ☐ Tights ☐ Stockings ☐ Strapless and push-up bra ☐ Thongs and boy shorts (no lace) ☐ Fitted jeans (dark denim or black) ☐ Robe ☐ Flip flops ☐ Shapewear (curvy models)	☐ Bottled water ☐ Hand sanitizer ☐ Toothbrush and toothpaste ☐ Mouthwash ☐ Floss ☐ Panty liners (full-size and thong) ☐ Stud earrings (no real jewelry) ☐ Safety pins ☐ Mini sewing kit (needle, thread, double-sided tape, buttons) ☐ Handheld mirror ☐ Book, earbuds, journal for free time
MALES				
☐ Shaving cream and razor ☐ Brush and normal hair products ☐ Unscented deodorant ☐ Baby oil, lotion or moisturizer		☐ Variety of shoes ☐ Dress shoes (casual and sport) *Colors: black, brown, and colored. Casual shoes can have design/trimming*	☐ Black fitted shirt ☐ White t-shirt ☐ 2 different colored jeans ☐ Dress shirt ☐ Fitted swim trunks ☐ Black boxer briefs	☐ Bottled water ☐ Hand sanitizer ☐ Toothbrush and toothpaste ☐ Mouthwash ☐ Floss ☐ Book, earbuds, journal for free time

Model Release Forms

A model release is handled before or directly after the shoot. It's a standard legal document between the photographer and the model that states who has rights to the images, the resolution, and what the images will be used for. It also should indicate the duration of the agreement and general purposes for using the images. I always recommend getting as specific as possible but, at a minimum, listing all general purposes. Example of specifics are if it's for portfolio images only or magazines only. This will help ensure you're getting paid properly if it is a paid shoot. If it's a TFP or a shoot you're paying for, it will specify what the photographer is using the images for as well.

Here is everyone's role in the situation:

Photographer: He/she owns full rights to the images, and they have the right to know what the images will be used for. They must provide company information on the document.

Model: Models under 18 must have a parent's or guardian's signature. Ultimately, the photographer owns full rights; however, he/she can give permission to the model or company to own the rights. The model must list contact information or agency information on the document.

Client/Agency/Company: They must be listed on the release at the time the model signs.

Important: If you don't have these in writing, you don't have rights to the photos. Yes, your photos can be sold, used for marketing, and anything else the photographer wants to use them for. Moreover, the photographer can sue you for making money on the photos or using them in a way they don't agree with.

If for some reason your photographer does not have a model release form, you can make one yourself and have them sign it. I don't want to see any of you being sued for this. If you have done shoots in the past without them, and they are photos you planning on using other than for self-promotion, contact the photographer and put a release form in place. Going forward, ask about model release forms at the time of booking. This is part of handling your business and bossing up.

Prior to the shoot, you will want to discuss the turnaround time on getting your photos back and how you will receive them. Will you receive them on a disc, emailed, or a link to download? What size photos are you getting, low resolution or high resolution? Low resolution is about 96 dpi; this size is mainly for online purposes (email, post, website). High resolution is 300 dpi; this is the size you need to be able to print a clear photo. If you try to print 96 dpi, the photo will look distorted.

Be sure the photographer keeps their word. You want to know this information before your shoot.

Lastly, if you're given permission to print your own photos, a photo release will come in handy. Some photographers do a model release and/or a separate photo release, and some just have it all on one document. A photo release is a document from the photographer showing that you have permission to print the photos. Some places will not allow you to print without proof.

Photo Shoot Evaluations

I talked about practicing, and now let's talk about evaluating. Photo shoot evaluations are a powerful best practice. Here's why: this gives you an opportunity to evaluate yourself and others. When you evaluate yourself, you see what you like and don't like and how you can do better the next time. It helps you improve, and it gives you a remembrance of how far you've come. Accomplishments are huge self-esteem boosters. I want you to grow after each shoot. Compete with yourself from shoot to shoot. You're only as good as your last photo.

So, starting with YOU first and then the others who are a part of the shoot, evaluating your team will give you a sense of whether or not you would work with them again and will help you to remember things you learned from them. Even when years go by, you will always have these evaluations to go to for reference.

Evaluation of Photo Shoot

Company Name:

Photographer Name:

Location of Shoot:

MODEL BEHAVIOR: **GET COACHED.** GET BOOKED. GET PAID.

Type of Shoot:

Date of Shoot:

Model Name:

MUA Name:

Hair Stylist Name:

Designer/Wardrobe Stylist Name:

Overall Rating of Shoot from 1–10:

Model Eval: Include your self-rating and overall performance, what things went well/what you can do better next time, what new things you learned, etc.

Photographer Eval: Include professional/unprofessional status, rating, comfort level, recommendation, etc.

Beauty Team Eval: Include professional/unprofessional status, rating, comfort level, recommendation, etc.

This evaluation is you evaluating you and making changes for better results. You can take a bold step and ask others involved in the shoot to evaluate you as well.

Selfie Challenge:

Selfie Challenge: Ladies, why does it take 10–50 selfies before we find one we like to post? And men, why do you hardly want to take one at all? It's because we are self-conscious about ourselves. Mentally we are thinking and talking, thinking and talking inside our heads without even saying a word out loud. Well some of us do; we let our thoughts come right out our mouth. It's almost like our thoughts are standing right in the middle of us and the camera.

Here's the challenge ... Take selfies doing facial expressions and send them to your best critics to see if they can guess your expression. Do not send a caption—you don't want to give them a hint. When you send them a selfie, you should get responses like "OMG, why do you look so sad?" or "What's wrong with you?" or "What are you so excited about?" I've even had models say some of them didn't text back; they called backed to see what was going on. You can do it ... GO!

STAGE 5
runway behavior

Let's get this straight right now: You must OWN the runway! Own it with confidence and like you can sell anything. Make your presence known from the time you enter until the time you exit the stage. People should feel your energy as you walk. You have to make them want to purchase the garments you have on right off your back even if they don't like them. Or get hired for another show or anxious to find out more about the designer and/or who you are. Give the audience something to see—they came for a show. This is the time you SHOW OFF!! Don't come out there like everyone came to see you take your first baby steps.

First and foremost, I need you to understand that models are hangers for designers. This is where the big disconnect comes in with some models. They begin to think it's all about them. NO, it's about the designer you're walking for. Models must understand that they are hangers for designers when it comes to the runway. You're wearing something that the designer has sketched, sewn, and created. Models are to display the designs in a way that they get sold. There is an entire team behind your overall look, including how your hair is styled and your makeup is applied.

So what is it that hangers don't do?

- Hangers don't TALK back to the designer, saying "I don't want to wear this" or tell the makeup artist the makeup is too much for you or the hairstylist that you don't like it—NO-NO.

- Hangers don't SIT without someone sitting them on a chair, meaning don't just sit down in designers' clothing without permission. You could be wearing satin material and when you get back up, the garment is wrinkled—NO-NO.

- Hangers don't EAT, yet there are models eating backing stage wearing designer garments or having food near clothing racks—NO-NO.

A hangers job is to hang clothes. When clothes are hanging in the store, it's a display for people to buy. Otherwise, everything would be folded. Runway models' job is to hang clothes on their body as a display for people to buy.

Have you ever seen a pair shoes, a jacket, or any item of clothing on someone and you gave them a compliment? Or even took it a step further and asked them where they got it? That person was modeling and didn't even know it. That person unconsciously made someone interested in purchasing the item. That's exactly what you want to do, but with a conscious effort. Every time you walk that runway: SELL, SELL, SELL.

The good news is that you're not just a hanger anymore, but keep yourself humble in this regard. Take that humbleness and still show up and be great! You're a brand; you're a BOSS, so when you speak, represent your brand well. When you walk, strut like a boss and handle your business like a CEO.

You learned how to walk when you were a baby. As the days went by you got better and better, skipping, jumping, and running around everywhere. You already have a unique walk about you. Check it out by using a body a mirror or recording yourself walking. Really look at your natural walk. Start your runway walk off by putting power behind your regular walk. Increase your energy level, focus, and start demanding attention with your presence.

Ladies First

I love using sketches and silhouettes for illustrations, because it causes you to focus in on the obvious that can be normally in disguise when it's dressed up. For example this sketch looks like a nice runway walk. However, she has what I call wide arms. Her left arm/our right is so far from the body that it becomes a distraction. I've seen some models' arms go so high they could have slapped themselves in the face. Wide arms come from the arm swinging from behind the body, the bouncing of the hip, or bending too much at the elbow. Another distraction is when the arms swing in front of the body back in forth. People's eyes will naturally zoom in on the arms and away from the garment. Let these runway diva techniques you'll read coming up, help your walk obtain the next level.

Runway Diva Techniques

Poise & Posture

- Stand up straight, lift your shoulders up, push them back, and bring them down. As your shoulders are coming down, imagine having bricks on your shoulders and elongating your neck at the same time.

- Tighten your abdomen and stand in a modeling stance. Imagine you're in the

inside of a clock, and your legs are used to tell time. Take your left foot and point it at the 12 and place your right foot behind your left foot pointed at the 3. Your feet will represent 3 pm and look like a capital "T."

Open Stance & Close Stance

- Both stances are the exact same model stance at the 3 pm position. The close stance is when the heel of your left foot is touching the middle of your right foot and your knees are locked. Use the close stance when you're in formal attire, like ball gowns, etc.

However, the open stance is the stance you're generally in when presenting yourself on stage. This stance is used from casual to couture looks. Just slide your left foot forward with a slight bend at the knee and shift your weight to the back, literally.

Crossover (one foot in front of the next)

- Your crossover should be tight. Start by practicing walking a straight line. Do this in slow motion. Bring your right foot off the ground and bend the knee slightly as you take a step forward. Before putting your foot on the ground, slightly move it over to go in front of the foot already on the ground. Then point your toes towards the ground and touch the ground toe then heel. Depending on the height of the heels, your heel may touch the ground before your toes. In this case, still do the motions of pointing toes and attempting to touch the ground with your toes first. Once you have slow motion down pat, start practicing at your regular pace. This will be part of the runway challenge.

Balancing

- This comes from old-school teaching from 40–50 years ago, but it's still effective today. It used to be grabbing a few encyclopedias and placing them on top of your head. Nowadays they don't produce encyclopedias like those anymore, as everyone uses the Internet instead. So, you can place a hardback book 8 x 10 or larger on the very top of your head and then take another hardback and place it on top of your head crosswise. Stack up 3–4 books depending on the weight going different directions and then work on your poise, posture, and crossover.

Walking in Heels

- Some of us start off very young walking around in our mother's heels fearlessly. Or maybe you never walked in heels, and it's like an uncomfortable nightmare. When I'm training people to walk in heels, their biggest fear is falling; but when you actually fall in heels, you're no longer fearful. When you have a fear like that, your body tenses up and can't be free to give it your all on the runway. This part of my coaching has models tripping and falling all over the place, but they get back up stronger and more confident. The more you practice and practice hard, you may end up falling—and that's okay. Get that out of the way now. Get back up and keep going.

I want you to get so comfortable with heels that it feels like a tennis shoe on you for as long as you can take it. Sleep in your heels overnight so your feet can swell. If you wake up in the middle of the night to use the bathroom or for any other reason, keep them on. Now, you may be in some pain, and that's what you want. The benefits are your ankles will strengthen, your feet will get acclimated, and it will train your mind to discipline your body.

Model Tip: New Heels

- Take them outside and scuff up the bottoms so you can break them in prior to needing them for the runway.

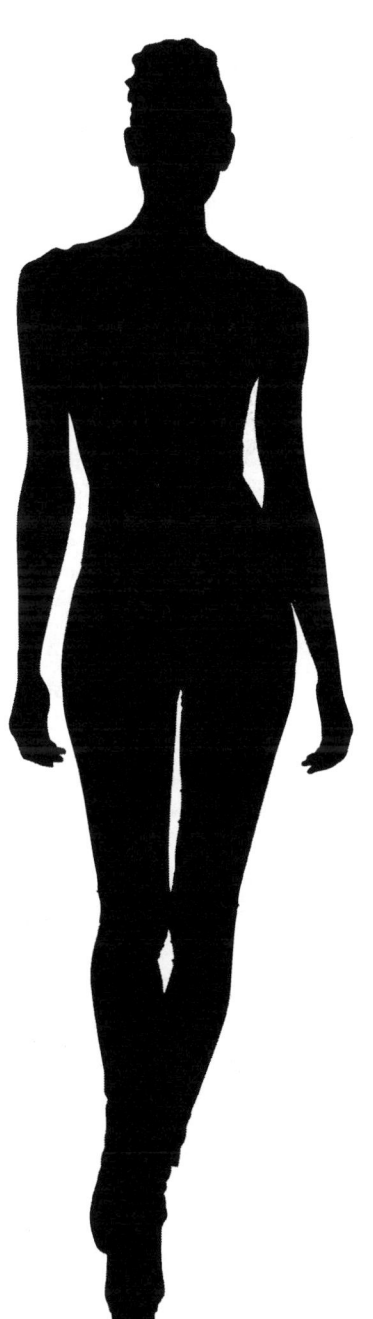

Invisible Heels

- Walk on your toes with the heels of your feet 3-4 inches off the ground. I have used this technique on the runway for swimsuit and lingerie collections. It gives a very elegant look versus walking flat-footed on the ground. This is one you may not need on the runway when you don't have on heels, but it surely gives your walk a nice glide.

DIVAS on the runway, catwalk, ramp, or any other nickname you want to call it. Please…OWN IT.

Pose & Picture

When you're walking the runway, it is not a race. Give the audience an opportunity to fully look at the garments you have on. Some models walk so fast it's like now you see me and now you don't. Once you get to the end of the runway, do very basic, simple posing like the ones in the picture. Remember, you don't want to do something distracting from your garments unless it's called for. Hold your pose at the end of the runway 3-4 seconds to give the photographer a cha nce to take your picture. This can vary depending on the designer and or the producer of the show.

Hey guys!

Even though male model walks aren't about the crossover, you still have to own the runway. Bring out your swagger.

Swagger Walk

Walk a straight line with only your left foot on the line. The right foot will be side by side as you move down the runway. Keep your shoulders back, and maintain good posture on the runway. Keep the natural swing of your arms. Try not to be to stiff, because it will give you a robotic walk; and try not to be too loose, or it will give you a bop. There is a walk that falls in-between the robot and the bop … it's Smoothness + Demanding Presence = Swag. Your walk should make all the women want you and all the guys want to be you … and buy everything you have on.

Which one of these silhouettes do you relate to the most and why?

Both female and male models must tackle these runway behaviors.

Entrance & Exit

- When you come on stage, act like you're entering on a stage inside of a stadium filled with people ready to hire you for the next modeling job. Be bold and demand attention with your presence.
- As you exit the stage, leave with your audience with a lasting impression of you, anxiously wanting you to come back out.

Eye level

Put your hand beside your eye pointing forward and then extend your arm, looking toward your fingertips. That's where your eyes should be at all times. Forward, even when you turn, don't drop your eyes.

When you look at the floor it shows a lack of confidence, and it's very distracting; and when you look up higher than eye level, you begin to take the life out of your face.

Strides

Long and steady strides look best. When practicing, imagine you're stepping over a puddle of water, give yourself some distance in between steps. Keep yourself standing tall and long. Baby steps are for babies.

Passing

This can vary based on producers and the size of the stage. In some shows you will

be far apart from one another on the stage, and in others you will be close and pass by using your shoulders. However, no one is going to want you to walk in front of each other to get by.

Walking with a prop
Props can be things that add to the overall look of the design, or a prop can be another person. The more props are involved, the more you have to show and tell without talking.

Runway face
Relax your mouth and keep it natural. Be cautious of fidgety movement with your tongue, a blank stare, and biting or licking your lips.

Everything is a runway: Start practicing using alleys, curbs, parking lots, etc. NO EXCUSES.

Now that we've got that straight, let's get runway etiquette understood.

Runway Etiquette
Have respect for the runway. Have respect for the entire team involved in the production and respect for the designers and other models. Here are some quick points for runway etiquette:

No gum or candy
This may calm models when they're nervous, but it's a big distraction to those looking at you. The focus shifts from the overall look to your gum chewing.

If you fall, get up.
Yes it may hurt and even feel embarrassing. If you get back up fast enough, some people might even miss it. Depending on the amount of time and space you have backstage, you may be able to do a walk backstage for a quick practice in your shoes with the outfit. I realize that the majority of models who fall on the runway either trip over the dress they're wearing or their pants leg is too long for the shoe. Sometimes even heels can get stuck in the runway.

No singing, including lip synching
I don't care if your favorite song comes on. DON'T sing it. Hum it if it gets you that excited. No lip movement outside of adjusting your facial expression unless the designer specifically asks you to.

Never walk to the beat.
If the music has a really fast beat or a really slow beat, don't try to keep up with it. You should have a steady pace when you walk with or without music.

Talking should be left backstage.
People are the #1 distraction for any model on the runway. It can be someone in the audience trying to get your attention. They could have a really big gesture or outburst. The photographer or media crew could be saying look this way. Even if that's the case and you can't figure out what they are trying to communicate to you, never give a response back from a live runway show.

Never run off the runway.
Even with a wardrobe malfunction, hold it, pull it up, and cover it or whatever you have to do for a temporary fix until you exit the stage. If it's that bad, model faster until you get to the end.

Always follow the direction of the director/producer or whomever in charge. For example, if they say curve off the runway at the end, don't turn around and pose.

Find a focus point without looking too high up. The higher you look up the more life you take out of your face and begin to go into a daze. Eye level is the best place to keep your focus, which is straight ahead.

Backstage

Backstage is extremely busy even if it's organized—and a lot crazier when its disorganized. It's very important that you are prepared mentally, physically, and emotionally.

Mentally you must have patience. Depending on how things are set up, you will have to go through hair, makeup, fittings with designers, and even a walk through of the show. Stay away from any negativity from others and even the negative thoughts coming from your own mind. It will bring stress and irritation.

What you can do in between fittings or while waiting, take out your pastime items from your model bag. Ear buds, a book to read, or your journal and think of a successful outcome for all parties involved.

Physically you must be prepared. Get plenty of rest one to two days before. You're going to need it. You may be walking for multiple designers back to back, lights beaning on you, adrenaline pumping, and your body feels like you're at the gym. There have been models getting extremely dizzy and/or passing out from hitting exhaustion. Before you know it, time has flown by and you still haven't eaten. With all the fast pace moments and excitement, you're burning calories. Your metabolism will be all over the place. Don't assume food will be available or healthy for you to eat.

Help yourself

- Pack your own lunch and include protein and healthy snacks; avoid salty foods.
- Water, Water, water.
- Watch out for the bloaters: dairy and especially bread and bananas

Emotionally, be powerful. This takes a beating the most because it's affected by both your mental state and physical state. If you really wanted to walk for a certain designer and you weren't selected or couldn't fit in the clothing the way they needed you to, it can affect your emotions tremendously and in a way that it changes your mood.

MODEL BEHAVIOR: **GET COACHED.** GET BOOKED. GET PAID.

Runway Workout

Ladies

Put a gallon of water in each hand and practice posture, arms, and walk.

Street lines are perfect for practicing your "Crossover & Stride" for the runway. Walk in straight line in between the yellow lines. For white lines, walk directly on the line since it's only one. The pedestrians and traffic is your audience.

At night when you sleep in your heels, I dare you to walk to the bathroom doing your runway walk, overcoming the pain from swollen feet in the middle of the night.

Guys

Incorporate 20 push-ups in between full walks up and back.

Modeling is not all glitz and glam, IT'S WORK.

Runway Model Challenge:

Practice at least 15 minutes a day on runway. Keep in mind that anything can be your runway: hallways, sidewalks, alleys, etc. Watch your favorite model on the runway and learn from them.

Test your runway self
Were you keeping eye level, arms beside you, walking a steady pace, and posing 3–4 seconds at the end?

[scam]

It happened to me one time, and I vowed never to let that happen again

STAGE 6
mmm: model coaches, mentors, & modeling schools

A **Model Coach** is someone who has extensive knowledge and experience in the modeling industry, who focuses on model development and helping models reach their full potential and exceed their goals. Model coaches intensely help models one on one to execute and deliver.

I became a model coach for these very reasons. It was time to take all of my knowledge and everything I have gained and pour it back into others. It's amazing to me to go through the growing pains and the wins with models, and it still brings joy to my soul. This book is offering you some of what you'll get in my coaching program, including model consulting and education. I'm talking strengthening your weaknesses and enhancing your strengths. I love coaching those ready to demand attention visually and internally to produce results in their lives through fashion. Get coached.

One thing I learned over time is that having a good coach is priceless. Coaches keep you focused on your goals and what's really important to you even in a world of distractions. Coaches are your biggest cheerleader, help you solve problems, encourage you, and become like family. I personally knew that I couldn't just do it on my own; I needed some help in the areas of my life that I was focusing on changing. I want to be the sharpest I can be. So now, I have several coaches, I'm where I need to be in my life, and I'm constantly exceeding far more than I did before I made a decision to get coaches in these areas. I will continue to add to this list of coaches until I have a coach for every aspect of my life. That's how much my life means to me.

I currently have the following coaches

- Life Coach
- Book Coach
- Fitness Coach
- Business Coach
- Spiritual Coach (pastor)

Everyone needs to consider having someone or a team/village in their life that has experience in the area they have most interest. Why? Because you can be setting yourself up to fail without any. As a child we are born to parents who are supposed to train us until we get old enough to know what to do. Some of us may have guardians or other family members who raise us. Whether for good or bad, these people are your coaches and role models. You need to learn from someone who has already been where you are and/or has the knowledge and experience to get you where you need to be. If you want to be a freelance model, that's fine; but I still recommend someone helping develop you to your full potential.

Coaches and mentors are similar in a few ways, but they are not the same. A Mentor is an experienced person who can lead, guide, counsel, and consult and advise you. This person is trustworthy and shares wisdom. One of the best things you can do for yourself is get a mentor.

Having mentors from a distance are impactful as well. These are people who aren't at arms' reach to call directly or just hang out over at their house. However, you can learn so much from them just by watching their life, studying them, and learning all you can just by doing that. I love me some Tyra Banks, Kimora Lee, and Kelly Cutrone. I have learned so much from reading their books and watching their shows and interviews, paying attention to their moves and respecting their stories. Just because I haven't talked to them directly, yet, has never stopped me from learning from them and applying it to my life. Call me crazy, but I have their pictures on my vision board, and one day I will thank them personally for all they have done to impact the lives of people they've never even met.

Think of it as someone who has paved the way driving through hurricanes and flying through blizzards. Now you have a smoother ride because of them; they can guide you in your long-term goals. Having a person to go to that can give you sound advice and lead you in the right direction, saving time and money, is priceless. Although a mentor is not there with you on a day-to-day basis telling you exactly what to do, step by step like a coach … a mentor plays a major part in your long-term development. The encouragement you receive and resources you tap into make a different.

Finding a mentor is like finding clothing you really like and buying it in the store without trying it on and then getting home and finding it doesn't fit or it's damaged. Now you have to take it back. Take your time looking for a mentor; nowadays even mentor programs are in place looking for mentees to help.

I use to think mentors were the hardest things to find. Back in the early 2000s, it wasn't anyone going against the industry standards and succeeding. I thought that there was no one to help me. At that time I was having limiting thoughts and holding myself back from getting a mentor. After getting past that, I started looking into the resources I already had, as well as resources from people in business and in fashion or modeling.

Who are your mentors? Who are your mentors from a distance? They are out here. This is another reason to create your goals. People aren't able to help you effectively if they are not sure where you're headed.

Some may ask, "Do I have to enroll in modeling school?" Nowadays, modeling schools have gotten themselves a bad reputation. The reputation came when schools were charging people thousands of dollars for information that people felt wasn't relevant. Some schools also made a lot of promises to those who signed up that they were going to make it, and when it didn't happen, the people who paid were upset. Many of the teachers didn't have much experience. There were modeling schools partnering up with agencies as way for both of them to make more money off the model. The agency would refer the model to the modeling school and have the model come back to agency once they finished paying for school. From there the school and agency get paid. Listen, that's business.

I worked at a modeling school back when I was 18 years old. I was so excited about helping people and learning more myself. They gave me very little training; thank God I knew a lot of the topics they were teaching already so that I delivered the best I could. The training they gave me was slim to none, and I realized I knew way more then the director of the school. This was crazy to me; how could I be learning anything new when I was teaching the boss? Next thing I knew, complaint after complaint was pouring in, and the staff was in a terrible position because so many people were dropping out because of the money. Staff turnover was crazy, so the models weren't able to build a rapport with their instructors. People had some really harsh things to say. I didn't believe all this was about money. Then one day I was in a staff meeting, and that's all that was discussed. Not who's doing well, badly, or needs extra help. Not how we were doing in our classrooms or if any of the staff needed extra help. No. It was about getting them to spend more money. I was the only one in the room letting them know that if we gave more attention, building to better them, they would want to spend more with the company. It kind of became a joke as the conversation continued. I was crushed to learn how they did things. Long before the program ended I wanted to quit, but I couldn't because of the kids I was teaching. They were depending on me. At the end of it all I was crushed again to find out that the list of agencies that was given to the students wasn't exclusive at all—you could simply look them up in the phone directory at that time, and today we have Google.

However, modeling schools have led to some success for both models and actors.

MODEL BEHAVIOR: **GET COACHED.** GET BOOKED. GET PAID.

The ones who brought down the reputation really made it bad for any good schools out there. There are modeling schools that are doing exactly what they said they were going to do in educating and developing talent.

People ask if it is a must to go to modeling school to be a model. No, it isn't; but you can learn a wealth of information, build experience, and become more confident by doing so. Just like coaching is a form of schooling, because you're being taught information. Whether you choose a modeling school or coach, I want you to think about what you're going to do become knowledgeable on a day to day basis about the industry you have chosen to work in. This is important.

Then you have your modeling troops, groups, squads, and organizations. Someone starts it up or a group of people start it and appoint a board of some sort. Years ago, these were considered entertainment models/hobby models. Entertainment models are models that mix the runway walk with dance movements, and it may or may not be about designer garments. They are there to entertain the audience, not to sell clothing. However, some groups have actually gotten paid to perform.

LISTEN, SCAMS ARE REAL, and they exist in every industry. In the modeling and fashion industry, people will pay a lot of money if someone tells them they could make them a star. No one can guarantee you tons of work, even supermodels' work can be inconsistent. If they promise you something, get it in writing.

Models become vulnerable when they don't research reputable companies and get their money taken. I got scammed one time, and I vowed to never let that happen again. I was 19 years old, and I decided to take an acting class. At this time I had a job, making my own money, so you couldn't tell me I wasn't grown. I signed up for class that was around $350.00. They gave people an option to break it up into two payments, but it was cheaper if you just paid in full.

I paid in full on my debit card, took the class, and that was it—well, I thought it was. About six months later I was checking my bank account and was upset, feeling like I should have more money than what I had. After checking the history, I couldn't believe what I was seeing. The SCAM company had kept charging my account for six months straight. After they had taken out the $350, they took $30 here, $80 there, $55 here, $130 there over and over and over for six months. Once I totaled it all, it was close to $1,500 bucks. This was an account I never really used; I would just make deposits so I didn't notice it right away. I was so angry, I took my bank statement and flew over there. Once I got there, I couldn't control myself. I was screaming and yelling all over the place. I told the owner, "What you're not going to do is turn me away until I get my money back … right now, today." I had the cops on speed dial, because I didn't know how this was going to end. They had messed with the wrong person—woo Chile! I showed them my statement, and they had a class about to start, so they kept trying to quiet me down, but apparently my vocals aren't set up that way. I had never heard of this scam before, where you keep charging people's cards different amounts; I was only 19. I said if you took $1,500 from me in the last six months and did the same to the other 10 people that took the class with me, that's $15k. Needless to say, I got my money back as well as the money from the class I had originally consented to pay for. One of the employees told me it was my fault for not checking my statements sooner. This was after the owner had refunded me. I went off again and said you're going to do that to someone and not have a business anymore. This was only one SCAM, but there are thousands of scams out there.

In short, if I had done my research, this would have never happened to me. I researched after the fact and realized it was in my face the entire time, but I didn't do what I call "pre-work." For you to avoid scams, it's going to take some work on your part before spending money.

Pre-Work—research online using the name of the company and keywords like scam, fraud, con, rip-off, and crooked agency/company.

Check Ratings—Yelp or similar sites are a good place to start to check reviews of the company before hand.

Ask for referrals or testimonials—These people should be visible on sites or social media. You can always inbox/dm them or ask around. People whose companies promote or said they have worked with the company/agency should always be accessible for at least verification purposes.

MODEL BEHAVIOR: **GET COACHED.** GET BOOKED. GET PAID.

Pay attention to RED FLAGS—for example, you have to work with their specific team of photographers or stylist, cash only for services, the offer is only available today, and promises to get you work immediately.

Don't throw away any of the paperwork, especially offers they make you.

Never, ever be pressured to do something or spend money quick. Go with your gut—if you're feeling something isn't right, chances are it isn't.

It's time to start making some decisions and taking control over your career. Plan out your future. If you desire to be signed with an exclusive agency, begin researching agencies that you may want to sign with. If you would like a non-exclusive agency, research them, and they can possibly help you get signed to an exclusive agency and offer recommendations. If you choose to remain a freelance model, become extremely familiar with all the roles agencies have that freelancers fill. Based on your ultimate goal, you can utilize resources and work toward your goal daily.

Just because people have negative things to say about modeling schools doesn't mean they're all bad. People say negative things about colleges they have had bad experiences with, but it doesn't mean all colleges are bad. Students are enrolling and graduating all the time with the degrees and bettering their lives. I always say DO YOUR RESEARCH before making a decision.

Do coaches and modeling schools cost? Yes, as do some mentors with programs. However, that's not a bad thing, because you're making an investment in yourself. Choose wisely. Education cost, programs, managers, and booking agents cost. As far as paying for education or some sort of personal training, we all have to understand that it's still a business at the end of the day, and there is a cost to running any business. It becomes a waste of money if a company isn't doing exactly what you're paying them to do. It's also a waste of money when you don't do your research or start but don't finish, or when you're not actually doing the things they are telling you to do, not taking it seriously, or expecting things to just fall in your lap without doing the work.

Are you worth your investment??

STAGE 7
agency vs. freelance modeling

Modeling is one giant community, but it's separated into these two categories that draws the line when you're getting booked and paid. After you read through this stage, I want you to combine the category you want to be in with the goal you started in Stage 1. That way you will have both what type of modeling you desire to do and what category you want to do it in.

Agency Model	Freelance Model
Exclusive Agency	Independent Model
Non-Exclusive Agency	Hobby Model
Mother Agency	Contracted Per Job

Agency Model: There are three core types of agencies. Exclusive, non-exclusive, and mother agencies. Research reputable companies; you want an agency that's going to advance your career.

- **Exclusive agencies** are the top agencies around the world that pay models a yearly salary to be signed in contract with them. This is where you will find your supermodels. They have the financial budget to afford to sign you and take care of all your expenses for you to become marketable, such as photos, training, traveling, image, etc. Agency models get paid more because major clients prefer to hire through a professional agency the majority of the time with assurance of the caliber model they are getting and not wasting time looking around and taking a risk.

As an **exclusive model**, you will NOT be able to book work or sign with any other agencies during the length of your contract. If an agency is exclusive but does not pay a yearly salary, you still are NOT able to work with any other companies.

- **Non-exclusive agencies** take up to a 20–25% commission fee for representing you/booking your work. However, being in a non-exclusive contract will allow you to sign with other non-exclusive agencies, find your own work, and book your own work without receiving commission. This can get tricky when the model finds their own work. The agency may feel they are entitled to a percentage. Please clarify during your contract negotiations.

  If you decide to sign with multiple non-exclusive agencies, have some reasons why—maybe different cities, targeting different clients or different categories from Stage 1. I say that because you don't want to put yourself in a position where you're getting over exposed before you're getting paid. The multiple agencies you're signed with can all be submitting you for the same job. If clients see your face everywhere, they may not book you for that reason. Clients love fresh faces. Keep that in mind.

- A **mother agency** is normally the agency you start out with when you first get into modeling. They may or may not have the financial budget to invest in you fully, but they can receive commission once you are signed to a bigger agency. Mother agencies can sell rights to another company and get paid. Mother agencies can also market you to exclusive and non-exclusive agencies and receive a finder's fee or commission after they help sign you to bigger agency for the duration of your new contract.

This is why you have to RESEARCH REPUTABLE AGENCIES and READ and have an attorney look over your contract. Don't just sign with an agency because they offered you a contact or because they are the only agency in your area. You can sign with an agency that's not in your hometown, but don't go by what someone else is telling you or what they are doing for another model. On top of a reputable company, get an agent who really cares about their models and is willing to do whatever it takes to advance their career.

5 Things to Look For in any Agency Contract

1. Length of contract (how many years upon signing is the contract valid)
2. Non-exclusive/exclusive
3. Agency commission/model salary
4. Repays for advancements by agency or model
5. In the event of breach of contract, what is each party entitled to? (Be sure that the model is NOT the only one who can breach the contract).

Understand this: It's extremely important for a model to have a great relationship with their agent. Your agent is responsible for your career. A model's success is an agent's success. Models must communicate with their agent at all times. Don't change your hair color, cut it, or do something drastic to your appearance without consulting with them BEFORE you do it. You may not want to hear it, but I'm serious. It can be a deal breaker for a job they've booked you for.

When I started Signature Ink Modeling Company back in 2002, we operated as a mother agency. Models would get their start here, and I was very protective as if they were my very own. As time went on, they became like family What makes us different is the development and marketing of models of all heights, shapes, and sizes. Not only that, the core principles they were taught is timeless. Those lessons still hold value today. I'm most proud of all of my successors. Those who were a part of the company who went on to become business owners, designers, stylists, or photographers.

Freelance modeling is where the majority of models start out. Once you decide to model and you don't have anyone representing you, you are a freelance model.

A freelance model is a model who works independently to book their own work. They market themselves, find casting, and take care of all of the business side of things. Freelance models can also seek help along the way by hiring a model coach, consultant, and/or a booking agent or manager. If they choose to seek help, normally they are paying a flat rate, monthly fee, or percentage. As your career begins to grow, it may become difficult to be independent and concentrate on being a model at the same time.

We discussed hobby models in Stage 1. A hobby model enjoys modeling and can be passionate about participating yet does not get paid for their services. Do not beat yourself up if this is where you are but don't want to be. The percentage of models randomly walking down the street and getting picked up by top agencies is next to none nowadays in the U.S. As a freelancer, you could be a hobby model at the same time, and that's okay as long as you are working on your plan.

Those contracted per job are models that receive a one-time contract to do one job. This is when a model goes into contract with a company one time. Once everything in the contract is complete and the model has gotten paid, the contract ends.

Here are some things you can do as a freelance model to build your portfolio and fashion resume as well as gain experience and get noticed:

- Compete in modeling contests
- Participate in local shows at schools, churches, and community events
- Go to casting calls and auditions
- Attend fashion events and network

Managers

Freelance models do have the option to have someone operating as their manager. This person must become extremely knowledgeable about the industry and how to manage your career. A manager will be used as a liaison between you and your clients as well as taking on some of the duties as an agent. Be cautious when choosing someone to put in this role, because this person will be speaking on your behalf and representing your brand.

Children 17 and under who are not signed with an agency typically have one of their parents, typically their mom, as their manager (that we call "momager"). I've seen this role go incredibly well and crazy bad.

The parents that can separate the business from the personal and still be supportive of their child are the most successful. It's hard to invest your time and money into your child, and then he/she doesn't get picked or you think they should have gotten more. If someone says something you don't like but you keep your composure and smile and turn around and encourage your son or daughter, great job!

The overly supportive parents want to support but can become overbearing for the child and/or the casting agent. Sometimes an overly supportive parent can unfortunately be a hindrance. Casting agents have very little time to get to know your child. You don't want the agents or casting directors not working with the child because they don't want to be involved with the parent. Parents also have to understand that they cannot be in all the casting rooms. Some make their children extra nervous or become a distraction. Also, you have to realize you may or may not be on every set.

On the other hand, unsupportive parents bring discouragement and negative energy that puts the child in a space where they can't grow in the industry. Your son or daughter may not ever reach their full potential without your love and support.

I cannot close out this chapter without mentioning talent agencies. This could be an option for those who are multi-talented and do not wish to sign solely with a modeling agency. Having a talent agent could get you more exposure in media, stage plays, videos, hosting, etc., because you would be considered an actor. There's more flexibility for those who desire to model, act, dance, and sing; however, modeling jobs will not be the primary focus/talent. Talent agents make between a 10–20% commission.

Eventually you will begin treating everything you do pertaining to modeling like a business. We will talk more about that in the business of modeling stage of the book.

Time to boss up

STAGE 8
casting behaviors

Castings to Go-sees to paychecks.

Castings can be done on location and/or online casting. This is when models are seen by the model scouts, booking agents, casting directors, designers, photographers, or other industry professionals selecting the models during the audition process. You'll notice "model calls" or "open calls" are other phrases used to describe castings.

Call Backs are the phone calls models receive if they have been selected or are invited to meet with a Go-see face to face after the client has expressed interest.

A Go-see is when a model is contacted to go in and meet with an agency/company one on one to determine if they get hired. If the model is selected, the next call they will receive is booking information. If you're with an agency, be sure to tell them that in the beginning.

If a casting or go-see is scheduled from 1–3pm, you should not arrive at 2:45. The rule of thumb is if you're on time, you're really late. You should get there 15 minutes before the casting starts as best practice.

Both castings and go-sees can select models on the spot and/or do call backs at a later date. Neither is obligated to contact models back if they aren't selected.

Make an impression on paper first

Take your time completing forms during castings. Some models aren't getting call backs because their forms are incomplete, not legible, or simply do not follow directions. Fill out casting forms/model applications in their entirety. Don't leave blanks for them to assume—say something. That's like someone asking you a question and you ignoring him or her. If it doesn't apply to you, put n/a. Read the directions slowly when filling out paperwork. Don't skim through; you miss things when you do that. If you're submitting online or filling out paper, take your time a finish it completely.

When you're a freelance model and you're looking to sign with an agency, find out the model requirements as to what they're looking for by doing your research. Some agencies have certain days/times once a week or once a month or quarter for new faces to come in to cast or drop off Comp Cards.

Some models think that in order to submit to an agency, you have to have a portfolio or Comp Card; that's not always the case. Top agencies want simple photos submitted to them. Clean face (no makeup) hair pulled back with either fitted clothing or swimsuit on against a white background. That white background can be the wall in your house, honey. The key to that is lighting—make sure it's lit. If you can afford a small ring light, get one. If I mention something you're not familiar with, please google it to get full understanding.

Here is a basic online model submission:

First & last name
Phone number
Email address
Country
Measurements/stats
Mini bio

Do you have representation?
Gender
Date of birth (DOB)
Upload pictures (3–4 photos of you full body, waist up, chin up, and shoulder/profile shot)

MODEL BEHAVIOR: GET COACHED. **GET BOOKED.** GET PAID.

Agencies are now asking for social media accounts, especially instagram. You want to send them to your business pages. We will talk about this in the branding stage of this book.

If your goal is to be signed to an agency right away, start submitting to them and send over ONLY what they are asking for. Know this is not the time for extra. FOLLOW DIRECTIONS. If the agency list says to submit a photo with hair pulled back, don't have it swooped in your face. Clean face with no makeup means absolutely no makeup. They don't want to see you all made up. If you send photos that are not in the description of what they are asking for, nine times out of ten they'll be deleted.

For castings for print work or runway shows, they may ask for more pictures and or a comp card or portfolio, depending on the client.

Know your measurements/statistics, we call it stats for short. If you don't know your measurements, go get measured. Any designer, seamstress, or fabric store can help you with this.

- Bust/chest
- Waist
- Hips
- Height
- Weight
- Shoe size

 If you want to measure yourself, grab a measuring tape and look at my Youtube video; I can show you how: **youtu.be/R58jKKL80gk**

Memorize your measurements; it can cost you a job.

Mini Bio

Here is a chance for the client to get to know you by what you write. For starters, think about the few words that best describe your personality (e.g., fun, outgoing, go-getter, etc.). Then think about some of the good feedback or testimonials you received from previous clients you worked with and/or impressive comments from others (e.g., pleasure to work with, punctual, creative, amazing, professional, etc.). Put it all together by creating three to four sentences top.

One best practice is to keep your bio in the notes on your phone or in your email to save time. That way you can always put your fingers on it when you need it. Make it good, but be honest about everything you write down and submit. You don't want any of this coming back on you.

Date of Birth (DOB)
Models cringe over putting down their age. Some feel they're too old and others feel they are too young. What really matters in this situation is how you look. You will find some castings are very strict on age requirements, just like height requirements, but don't let that stop you. Be honest.

List of Experience
Some model applications that don't ask for bios may ask you to list your experience. Put down the top 3-4 things you've done. You can throw in recognition only if its something relevant to modeling—like featured in a particular magazine, fashion week, or print advertisement—but don't write it in a way that seems like you're tooting your own horn.

Now that you have made an impression on paper first, know you need to be prepared.

10 Things you should do when preparing for a casting:

1. Wear clean and comfortable shoes.
2. Wear your smile.
3. Check your confidence and your energy level prior to going; have a winning attitude.
4. Go to the location prior to the date to see exactly where it is.
5. Arrive 15-20 minutes early even if the doors aren't open.

6. Have marketing materials ready: Comp Cards, portfolio, tearsheets, business cards Check for wrinkles, tears, or bends in photos, etc weeks before. They should be clean and sharp.

7. Research the company to make sure this is the job you want.

8. Go to castings/go-sees with a purpose.

9. Follow directions on what they ask you to bring.

10. PRACTICE*ALWAYS*

These 10 easy things make all the difference. If you miss these, you may not have the best day.

It's natural to feel nervous going out to castings; the thing is that when you constantly think about it and say how nervous you are it turns into fear. Fear will keep you from being at your best and even scare you out of attending. Your fear might not go away, but the opportunity will. Make the choice to be fearful or fearless.

What to wear to castings?
All Black Fitted Clothing. I call this the model uniform. You can wear this on castings, go-sees, backstage, fittings, etc. Every model should have black in their wardrobe.

On rare occasions clients ask for you to wear skinny jeans and a fitted top or a fashionable outfit. In this case, always follow directions, of course.

Do castings cost?
No, you shouldn't have to pay to attend castings. And you shouldn't have to pay for an agency to take a look at you or to be signed with them.

Can I bring people with me?
No boyfriends, girlfriends, kids, or anyone else should be in the casting room with you unless you're under 18. They can wait outside, on the other side of the door or in a totally different room. Note, I said casting room, they can still be in the building.

Professional Pictures

I love all of our new camera phones, and some tablets have very good quality photographs. Some photos you take in front of really great scenery or with good lighting turn out great! Even using the filters on your phone to enhance the finished photos can be good. However, these photos should not be on your Comp Cards or portfolios, as they are not professional photos and should not be used to represent you in the modeling industry. Printing phone pictures can be low resolution or even pixelated. You want the best quality photos possible to represent you. Remember, a picture says a thousand words and in those words; it will say whether you get the job or not.

There are 5 key elements to a great shot that each model must be engaged in to do. Next are 5 KEY COMPONENTS TO A GREAT SHOT.

Models often ask what can they do if they are just starting out modeling or have been modeling for some time but no one has expressed interest. No matter how it seems, build your team. Be consistent and don't give up.

The "G" (glam) Team (People involved in the shoot)

- Model—YOU
- Makeup Artist (mua)
- Hair Stylist
- Clothing Stylist/Designer
- Photographer
- Bonus: Creative Director

Please understand that it takes each of these five areas to do 20% a piece to produce a flawless photo. If one of these areas is lacking, it could really hinder the results of your shoot. Just think about, what if everything was immaculate, but your makeup was three times lighter than your body or the lighting of the photographer produced really dark photographs. It would even be worse if your hair wasn't right or, if you're a male model, your shape-up was crooked. The shoot would be horrible. It's not just what the team does that can hinder a shoot. The model alone can make or break the shoot. A model can struggle with posing or feel uncomfortable with her wardrobe and not be able to deliver—then the shoot fails. If you're in a position where you have to build your own team, build the best team possible. Get the best photographer, makeup artist, hair stylist, and designer in your area. If you don't have a budget yet, you can start with asking to do TFP with photographers, makeup artists, hair stylists, and designers. Just keep in mind what we discussed in Stage 4. It's a 50/50 risk, but it can be beneficial for you. Select a fashion photographer and a team that specialize in fashion. You're not looking for an events team or those specializing in bridal. Give yourself the best chance at a flawless photo.

If you get some great shots, use the best ones for your portfolio or to evaluate yourself to do better. Treat everything you do in this industry seriously. Whether you're practicing on your own or TFP. Treat each time as if you're getting paid.

Your model **Comp Card** is like your mini double-sided snapshot portfolio. Some call it your oversized business card. Headshot on the front and 3–4 photos on the back with your name, stats, and agency information or freelancer info. I train models to target their client on the back photos. That means only put photos related to the clients you're trying to attract. If you want to be a commercial model, put commercial photos; if you want to be a specialty parts model, then put parts on your Comp Card. If you have more than one client you want to target, then put one photo representing each client. Comp Cards should be updated every 9–12 months or if the model has had drastic changes, such as weight loss or gain, haircut or color, or a change in target client. There isn't a right or wrong to the layout of your card or design of the card. The average size is typically a 6 x 8 with a very basic design to prevent distracting from your photos.

Your Comp Card is what is sent out or given at castings to agencies and industry professionals. Your Comp Card is normally what a client sees before they meet you. When selecting your comp photos, you have to think about your comp on the table with 50 other models. Your photos have to make the client pick your card up and turn it around to see more of you. This Comp Card speaks for you, and if the photos aren't up to par, it will get tossed. If your card is selected, next will be a call back to see the client or a go-see, and then your portfolio comes into play. Never send your actual portfolio book to a client or leave at a casting. If the client already has your Comp Card and wants to see more, you can send them to your website, which is your online portfolio. We will chat about that more in the branding stage of the book.

Agency models Comps are different, agencies' information will be listed on only, and they will make the decisions on photo selection.

Your **Model Portfolio** is an unfinished book of your work. I say unfinished because you should always be working and moving new photos into your book and old photos out of your book. Each shoot should get better and better, especially if you're evaluating it like I told you about before. If your aren't signed to an agency at the time you start your portfolio, keep it updated. Some agencies will even tell you to come back after you build a portfolio. That means they do see potential but aren't willing to take a risk on you just yet. It can be a little misleading, but just because they tell you that doesn't mean they will cover expenses or reimburse you.

When starting your portfolio I want you to keep in mind it's all about quality and not quantity. I would rather you have 4 shots giving tens across the board than 20 shots giving threes.

Portfolio Do's

Before starting your portfolio, I want you to start with a plan and then work the plan.

- The first thing I would like you to do is purchase the portfolio book. Some places will have it listed as an art book. Standard size is 8 x 10 and other sizes are 9 x 12 and 11 x 14. Keep in mind that the larger the book, the more expensive the overall printing will be. Larger books are a great way to display images in your book. However, get what you can afford.

- Create a photo idealist. Think about the type of images you want to go in your book based on the clients you want to work for or agency you want to sign with.

- Start contacting your "G" teams and begin your shoots.

- Once you have evaluated your shoots, take the best photo from each shoot to put in there. You don't need 3–4 photos or the same exact look. Just the one best shot of the entire shoot. Every image in your portfolio should be an entirely different look. This means different outfit, different location, different pose, and different hair and makeup.

- Arrange your photos in such a way that you WOW your potential client. Keep them wanting more. If they open the book and your first shot is bad, they will close the book and give it back to you. The other thing is don't have 40 images or a bunch of the same looks such that they get tired of turning the pages—that's sign of a poor portfolio. 4–5 flips of the pages is perfect; that's 8–10 total different looks.

- Keep all vertical images together and all horizontal images together. That way the client can flip from vertical to horizontal view on time and not back and forth.

- Have a variety of shots in your book showing your range. It shouldn't be a book full of headshots or all full body shots. Have a combination of headshots, three quarter length and full body shots. Also, have different on-location shots and studio shots. You will need to use more than one photographer/"G" team to show variety as well.

- Retouching photos will be needed. This helps your photo go from a 6 to a 10. Your photographer should know how to retouch or have someone on his or her team that does. If not, make sure your model release says you can have someone else alter original photos.

When starting a portfolio start with your basics:

- Striking headshot (beauty shoot, very clean and natural looking)
- Full-length body shot (form-fitting clothing showing your body shape)
- Swimsuit (in studio)
- Commercial look

- Editorial look
- Striking closing shoot

If you have these shots above, go to your photo idealist to continue building your portfolio. You can use more of the editorial and commercial concepts but with different wardrobe. Other looks can be formal, sports, three-quarter length advertisement pose, shot with another model, accessory headshot, high fashion, automobile, etc. Go back to Stage 4 and review the notes on preparing for the shoot. This will help.

Tearsheets are the actual torn out magazine pages or publications that you have been featured on. These can be added to your port to show you have been published.

If you have already started your portfolio, ask yourself if you need to start again. Such as if your images aren't a 10, they don't reflect your current look, they're all similar looks, etc.

Portfolio Don'ts
- Don't put runway pictures in your portfolio if it's not a recognizable (well-known) show. No name shows in your port can downgrade you.
- Don't have photographer logos/copyright on the front of the image. Speak with the photographer prior and/or have it noted on your model release.
- Don't put personal pictures in your port, even if you rate it a 10. If it's not for modeling, put it in your personal home album.
- Don't have outdated photos dominating your port. All photos in your portfolio should not be more than a year to a year and half old.

Contact my office if you need additional help on Comp Card/portfolio materials, layouts, and/or images.

Note: Very few clients are taking digital portfolios on your ipads/tablets. Cell phones are just too small to show images; I wouldn't chance it. Clients still want to see how serious you are by the investment you've made in yourself. As time goes on digital portfolios may get popular, but right now old-school black portfolios are still the wave.

Modeling is the Beauty and the Beast, not just a pretty or handsome face. Know what you're signing up for … it's not always a walk in the park. From the outside looking in, people see all the amazing photos, are attracted by the beauty and concepts, and feel they want it too—and that's okay. You just have to know the reality behind it all.

Know that you can be on set for 10 hours without food. You can go to castings and go-sees for 8 hours a day back to back and get a bunch of No's. Standing too long, sitting too long. Limited space. Feeling tired, frustrated, and annoyed. Some of the best photos maybe taken in someone's basement or living room. You have to be open to different environments. Some of the best shoots are not necessarily where you're treated like a queen or king or some sort of celebrity. All of a sudden it's not as beautiful as you thought it would be. You have to want it but understand everything that comes with it.

Freelance models will have to pay for portfolios, Comp Cards, and branding materials if no one else does. Look at it as an investment in yourself and that you will make your money back. It's important that you are shooting with the best teams, like we discussed before, so you're not wasting time or money.

Castings can build your self-esteem or rip you apart. This is why you have to build your own self-esteem on a daily basis (MDI in Stage 1). Before going on a casting, prepare yourself for rejection as well as for being selected. Both of these are equally important, and here's why. Once you're selected, you have to deliver on the job. Are you ready? Once you're rejected you still have to smile and say thank you and walk away confidently. Are you ready?

Let's talk about the ugly side of castings. For example, you have everything prepared and you're ready, you audition, and they immediately say NO or you're not what they are looking for. Sometimes you don't get any response at all during the time of the casting and don't receive a call back. You are left feeling hurt, embarrassed, worthless, confused, angry, ugly, and so many other things. It all comes down to

REJECTION. Rejection is the dismissal or refusal of something. Knowing how to deal with rejection is going to be very important.

Dealing with rejection is very challenging. Starting with your self-esteem level. No one can give you self-esteem but you. That's why it's called self-esteem, because it comes from one's self. Confidence, on the other hand, is built by those around you who give you compliments and validation. Once you have those level up, then I want you to get an understanding of these emotions by knowing how to deal with them. Hurt, embarrassment, anger, etc. all have in common one thing—they're temporary (and negative). It's going to sting momentarily, but it will go away if you don't hold on to it. The benefits of overcoming rejection are your real break through. We will talk about that in the next stage.

When you go to castings, you are representing your agency and/or your brand. Know that everything you wear and things you bring with you, including the people you have around you, are representing you. Make sure you're sending the right message.

Casting Don'ts
- Chew gum or eat food
- Leave without saying thank you
- Be loud
- Bring company
- Have your phone sound on
- Be unapproachable
- Arrive late
- Try to do anything to get the job, such as being seductive, putting others down, buying your way in, sleeping your way in, lying, or cheating.

Note: When you go on a casting, you should be checking out the company as well to see if it's a good fit or not. If they ask you if you have any questions, ask them something. Come with at least one question in mind to ask. If you're not given the opportunity to ask question, you can ask one of the staff members on the way out or email if it's that important. However, you have the right to turn down a job. Agency models check with their agency prior to turning down a job.

In between castings and go-sees and shoots, keep yourself moving forward. Keep building, studying, and promoting yourself until you get where you want to be.

STAGE 9
benefits of overcoming rejection

Rejection can be harmful to your self-esteem if you allow it to. You allow it by continuing to run the same thoughts through your head over and over again—feeling the same pain of hurt, disappointment, being unwanted, and like you aren't good enough. Many tell you how to deal with it, but not how to overcome it.

Overcoming rejection is like being on a emotional rollercoaster. Initially you may experience fear, anxiety, depression, denial, loss and tears before you get to relief, excitement, happiness, laughter, and joy.

There were celebrities in the fashion industry that I had the chance to have actual conversations with about the lack of opportunities for models of different heights and sizes and mixed-race woman and men in the modeling industry. They told me it would never work, don't reinvent the wheel. There was no way they would even take a look at the models if they didn't fit the "industry requirements."

I remember letting that rejection lead me into a pit, time after time after time. The last time I let rejection get me so far into a pit, I couldn't seem to get myself out of the slump. I felt so low for so long that being angry and bitter and sad and depressed was becoming normal for me. Honestly, it took some time, maybe almost a year, to get fully out of my own pit of rejection. What was happening was the longer I was upset about it, the more I would attract rejection to myself.

Once I finally overcame the rejection, there was NO way I was going back in. I began to train my thoughts to reject the rejection. HA!

Your benefit comes from how you RECEIVE life or what happens to you.

It's the things we tell ourselves that carry the most weight, such as your thoughts. We have to accept that we are not going to be what everyone is looking for, and that's okay. Begin to train your mind now, by telling yourself that it's okay and reminding yourself that you're "fearfully and wonderfully made." If someone says you're ugly, it doesn't matter; what matters is if you tell yourself you're ugly and believe it. If someone says you're never going to make it, it doesn't matter; what matters is if you tell yourself that and believe it. The relationship you have with yourself determines where you will go in life. If you keep letting yourself down, allowing rejection to define you and break you down, your pit will end up like a black hole.

What you say to yourself is what you receive, and then you experience the shift.

Knowing your worth and loving yourself unconditionally is what matters. Don't stay in the emotions of feeling rejected; you don't have to accept that feeling in your mind and body. There is an opposite to everything in life.

Know this … Your mind is a powerful space. This is where you can create, experience, destroy, and reject things with your thoughts alone. Stay with me on this one.

That means if you want to create something, do it from in your mind first. If you want to reject something, do it in your mind first. Think of the outcome you want, create the outcome you want, and experience the outcome you want all in your mind first.

Here's what normally holds us back: FEAR. Sometimes fear makes us feel like little kids again, needing to sleep with the lights on because we created a boogieman in our heads. Fear has us afraid of stuff that may never happen. We have been using our powerful space against ourselves.

I love how the urban dictionary points out that fear spelled backwards is "raef"—the art of being able to excel in almost everything by being you. Replace your fearful thoughts, negative thoughts, and rejection thoughts. They're building bars to a jail in your mind.

Then there is inadequacy that makes us feel like it's a shortage of work, and limitations begin to jail in your mind. Know that you are enough. There is only one you, and you are enough.

Also, there's something about embarrassment that makes you wants to run and hide somewhere. Think about this, when someone says something to you in front of other people, you receive it totally different from when they say it directly to you when no one is around. That's because we care more about what others think of us and what others are saying about us than what we think of ourselves and what we say to ourselves. Take some time in your powerful space and replace those thoughts.

The feeling of being unwanted by some is normal, just as that of being wanted by many is normal. Which one will you make your normalcy? You can choose or let it choose for you.

If you're reading this book, you have already been rejected at some point of your life. You either went through the emotional roller coaster or you dealt with it by accepting it or just living with all of the emotions. Focus on the benefit of the fact that for every time you're rejected, there is a yes or two. You've been through all of these emotions, and the good thing is that you got through it. The key is don't keep going through it; get off that roller coaster.

Sometimes believe it or not rejection happens to strengthen you—when you get mad, you get aggressive. There is a feeling inside of you that makes you want to do more. That's good when it's working on the positive end of things, but not on the negative end. Using the energy of rejection for the negative is heading toward a train wreck.

Then you have the "what ifs." Right before and also afterwards. What if I don't get picked, but what if I do? What if I look crazy doing it, but what if I don't?? Stand in your greatness!

Validation is beneficial when you practice at something, study, fail, and try over and over again. Our human nature wants us to depend on others to be our validation, but we validate our own selves when we set a goal and accomplish something, when we keep to our commitments and when we study to show ourselves approved. Our confidence shoots through the roof, and we gain self-awareness.

Lastly, I want to give you one of my favorite quotes from Jack Canfield: "When they so No, you say Next." Baybeeee, I shouted and flipped everywhere when I got this revelation. I must have entered that into my powerful space 1000 times and said it more times than I know. There's FREEDOM in the word Next. Try it next time rejection comes.

And I say do this immediately. Don't spend time processing it. Don't get me wrong—if you are in a competition, the results from the competition are available, and you want to know your results, by all means do so when you can receive it and work from it.

When they say No you say Next.

It doesn't matter whether it's the casting, the job, seeking help, etc. Say NEXT.

Your benefit is in the NEXT, and if the next one says No, then it's in the NEXT one after that.

The Benefits of Overcoming Rejection

- Receive life by what you tell yourself
- Gain self-awareness through your powerful space
- Experience a shift
- Raef
- Gain self-awareness through self-validation
- FREEDOM

Reject the rejection, and be unstoppable

STAGE 10
image is power

On your mark. Get set. SLAY.

This is the top industry when it comes to visuality. Don't kid yourself into thinking anything different. You must care about the way you look, how you present yourself, and how you carry yourself. It's a must. This industry has a slew of models coming and going, auditioning all the time.

We discussed how to dress for castings in a previous stage, but now be informed about your overall image—how you can change or adjust to enhance your natural beauty.

First and foremost you should always be wearing your CONFIDENCE, or should I say GODfidence. Being attractive starts internally first. How you feel about your image plays a major part in how others look at you and can definitely be a deal breaker for clients to pay you.

Looking good and feeling good are so magnetic. You do this by being the best you that you can be. Have you ever seen yourself at your best? If yes, I know you loved you. I want you to have that same feeling all the time. Even if that means you have to get a makeover or, what I like to call it, an image enhancer. No, I'm not talking about getting a booty or boob job. An image enhancer is taking your natural look and increasing it to a level that showcases you visually at a 10. This means you may have to cut your hair, dye it, put in extensions or destroy weight, gain weight, dress differently or just have a total opposite look than what you're used to. Guys, as well, may need to cut their hair off or grow it out some to enhance their image. It's not the end of the world; it's actually the beginning of a different one. Some of you may already have had an image enhancement and don't even realize it. Others may need to get one, and some are so used to their look they refuse to change or struggle with the idea of change. You have to be willing to change.

This is when you have to boss up. PERIOD.

Get an understanding of what needs to be change to support your image enhancement—starting with your face shape.

Face shapes

This will help you determine the hairstyles and makeup that look best on you. If your aren't able to identify your face shape by the description, feel free to use a measuring tape or ruler. Measure the parts of your face from top to bottom starting with the length from forehead to chin. Then measure the widths of your brow, cheekbones and jawline. You'll find that some of your measurements maybe the same or close in numbers. Use the visual and description below to help you identify yours. Try the hairstyles described under the "Test the Best" sections and begin bringing power to your image.

MODEL BEHAVIOR: GET COACHED. GET BOOKED. **GET PAID.**

Oblong and Rectangular Face Shapes

Both oblong and rectangular face shapes are long and get slender by the jawline. From the cheekbones up to the forehead is just about the same in width. Foreheads may appear higher. The only difference is that oblong chins can be very narrow/pointy.

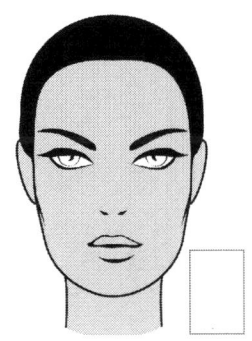

Test the Best

Choose short to medium length cuts that bring balance to the long and slender face shape. These types of cuts will you give width that adds volume to the sides of your face for perfect balance. Best styles are bobs to the jawline, layers, bangs, and curly and wavy styles.

Try To Avoid

Hair longer than your shoulder can harm your look. It will actually make your face look even longer than it is. Too much height at the top like top knots will add length to your face. Remember, never add length.

Celebrities with Oblong/Rectangular faces are Gisele Bundchen, Janet Jackson, Sarah Jessica Parker, and Denzel Washington.

Round Face Shape

Your face is generally as long as it is wide or close in numbers, with a round chin and hairline. Your face is full, with the widest points being the ears and cheeks.

Test the Best

Long hair, don't care.. for a round face shape. You can rock long length, long layers, and long curls as well as side parts with lengths longer than your chin. Layering the top gives you more fullness and having the rest of the hair close your face will cause it to appear longer.

Try To Avoid

...thick bangs, medium length cuts that end at your chin, and tight curls.

Celebrities with round faces are Cameron Diaz, Nicki Minaj, and Jack Black.

Square Face Shape

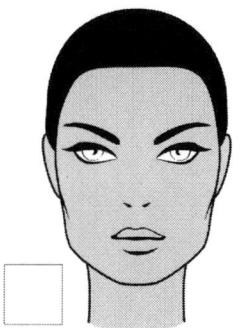

Measurements are the same as those for round but yours are angular features with a strong square jaw line and sharp cheekbones.

Test the Best

Go for softness towards the top of the head to balance a square jaw. Waves and curls add femininity to your look. Off-center parts keeping height in the crown area of your head as well as layers and shaggy and wispy looks around the face work well.

Try To Avoid

Long straight styles will accentuate the square jawline. Center parts, straight bobs, or cuts stopping at the jawline will not enhance your look.

Celebrities with a square face are Heidi Klum, Raven Symone, Demi Moore, and Brad Pitt.

Inverted Triangle Shape Face

This face shape is exactly like heart shape but without the peak at the forehead. I call this one the cousin of the heart shape. It's wider at the forehead, and the jawline and chin come to a slender point.

Test the Best

Bang! BANG ... this face shape can wear a bang that sits perfectly without the widows peak for those who want to disguise their forehead. Try a middle part with a half up-do and back down. A choppy or wavy bob with bangs and layers works well. Diagonal side parts, with swoops towards the ears will keep your face shape balanced.

Try To Avoid
Stay away from styles that will make your forehead appear wider and your face longer, like long straight styles, really short cuts, and hair pulled completely back.

Celebrities with inverted triangle faces are Tyra Banks, Jennifer Aniston, Iman, and Ryan Gosling.

Heart Face Shape
The key features here are the pointed chin, wide cheeks, and broad forehead with a peak.

Test the Best
Go for cuts that bring attention to your eyes and cheekbones. A chin-length bob will create balance by giving your face a fuller look. Side parts with longer styles, layers around the face and wispy bangs work well. If you decide to wear shorter styles, leave the weight of the hair in the back.

Try To Avoid
Top-heavy looks with height in the crown or heavy bangs will emphasize the upper part of your face, leaving the rest of your face looking extremely narrow down to the chin. Slicked back looks and short cuts that have tapered necklines will leave your face looking unbalanced.

Celebrities with heart shaped faces are Halle Berry, Naomi Campbell, Reese Witherspoon, and Leonardo DiCaprio

Diamond Shape Face

The widest part of the face is prominently the cheekbones. The forehead is narrow and almost the same in width as the jaw line.

Test the Best

If you're a true diamond, almost everything works on your face. Try a variety of styles and see which one you feel at your best wearing. With dramatic cheekbones you can go short; however, be sure to leave the weight of the hair in the back for a balanced look.

Try to Avoid

Styles that cover your good features. This is the face with which you can wear everything, so don't cover it up with hair. If you want the most attention on your cheekbones or eyes, try bangs.

Celebrities with diamond shape faces are Madonna, Serena Williams, Nicole Kidman, and Johnny Depp.

Triangular Face Shape

This is the reverse shape of the inverted triangle, with a sharp jaw line, narrowing in at the cheekbones to the temples. The jaw line is the widest part of your face and your forehead is narrow.

Test the Best

Short hair cuts that balance the jaw line like a sexy pixie cut or diagonal bob work well as do shags and lots of layers that give fullness to the upper part of your face. Side parts and tucking hair behind your ears will bring attention to your eyes. Buns! You can do a variety of buns and pulled-back styles as well as thick-banged ponytails, half up-dos, beachy waves, and sleek layers.

Try to Avoid
Long and full hair styles that draw attention to your jaw line and haircuts that elongate the top of your hair and the crown of your head.

Celebrities with triangular face shapes are Kathy Ireland, Victoria Beckham, and Justin Timberlake.

Oval Face Shape
Shaped like an egg with rounded chin and hairline. Your face is longer than it is wide.

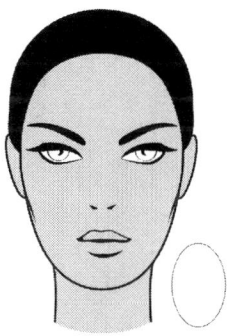

Test the Best
This is THEE face that can do short to long and everything in between. Your face shape is well portioned out, so go experiment with all the latest trends.

Try to Avoid
By covering your face with hair too much you'll begin to lose the shape of it.

Celebrities with oval face shapes are Beyoncé, Kimora Lee, and Matt Damon.

Note: As you transition to the best hairstyles for your face shapes, try wigs first if needed.

Men have the same face shapes but with stronger builds. Follow the same descriptions to identify your shape and note the celebrities listed to relate.

I threw face shapes for shades in here for you for when you're out and about or headed to casting. Have on some shades that fit.

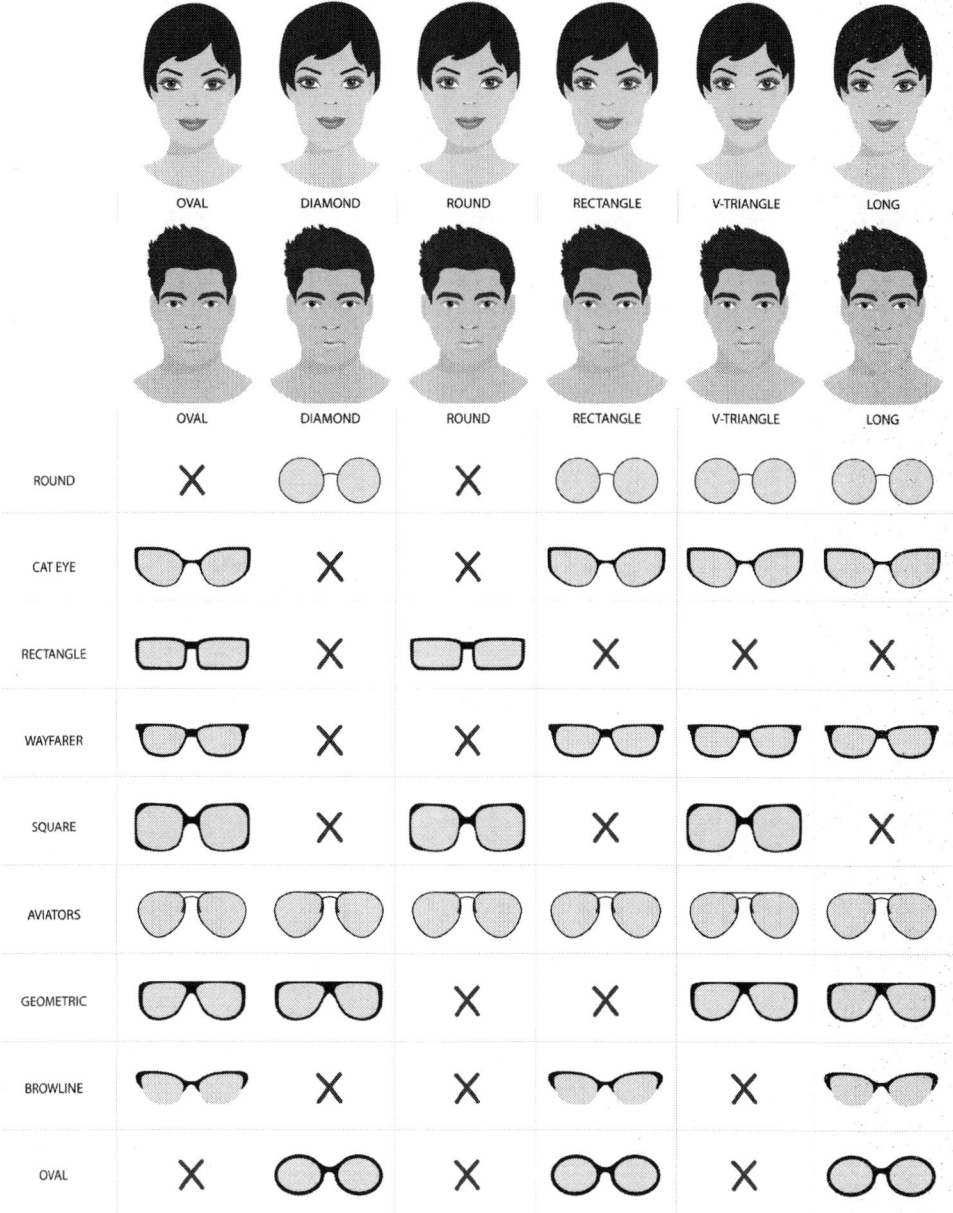

MODEL BEHAVIOR: GET COACHED. GET BOOKED. **GET PAID.**

Body shape is just as important, because sometimes we don't know or understand what that means. Of course people love the new trends, but not all of them may be the best for your shapes. What looks good on one person doesn't mean it will look good on you. You want what will look good on you and show your shape so that your image will speak POWER.

Let's get this out the way first.

Muffin top ... STOP IT!

Pear, apple, hourglass, and banana female body shapes.

Pear Shape

The majority of your weight falls below the waist.

Dress Your Best

Pear-shaped women should focus attention on the upper half of their body.

- Start with fitted tops. Jackets and tops that stop at your hips emphasize your defined waistline. Choosing slim, fitted tops and button down shirts and cardigans is best.

- A-line dresses, peplum tops, and jackets emphasize the upper body while slimming wider hips.

- Keep the hems of pants, skirts, and dresses wide to visually balance a pear-shaped body.

- Pointy-toed shoes with wide-hemmed pants will elongate your legs.

Bypass: Tops and jackets that stop at the waist will bring attention to the largest part of your mid section and may not give your shape the best look.

Apple Shape

The majority of your weight falls above the waist.

Dress Your Best

Apple-shaped women should focus attention on the bottom half of their body.

- Elongate your upper half by finding V-necks that lengthens your top. Go bold in trying different colors and patterns with silk and chiffon materials.

- Monochromatic outfits give length and have a natural slimming effect on your apple-shaped silhouette with the same color on top and bottom. Also, you can mix up varying shades of the color and different fabric combinations.

- Short dresses and skirts create an hourglass shape. Add a belt for even more slimming definition to your waist with a belt over a dress or long blouse.

- Boot-cut pants, flat front pants, and ones that button on the side as well as A-line skirts give a leaner look.

Bypass: Straight skirts from the waistline down and pants that are too tight will make your upper body look larger it is.

Hourglass Shape

Bust and hips are around the same size. There is normally a nine-inch difference between the waist and bust. Less than 10% of women have an hourglass shape. This shape is opposite of most supermodels.

Dress Your Best

Having a round and curvy shape with a well-defined waistline doesn't call for much to do. Look for clothes that silhouette your figure rather than hide it.

- Simple dresses, one pieces, and wrap-style skirts/dresses will showcase your small waist.

- Choose scooped neck tops and V-necks and tops with belts or ties for an even more slender waistline. Vertical stripes will elongate you.

- Fitted pants or those with a slightly flared bottom as well as low-rise pants work well.

Bypass: Ruffles, big bows, baggy bottoms, turtlenecks, and bulky fabrics.

Banana/Rectangle Shape

Undefined waist, narrow hips, and small bust forming the same width throughout the shape.

Dress Your Best

- Create curves.

- High-neck tops give the look of a fuller chest as well as scoop-neck tops.

- Belt your waist to create an hourglass shape.

- Coats and tops that flare out from the waist and stop at the hips will give the illusion of wider hips.

- Pleats, mermaid dresses, and layered skirts help give a bulky balance. Pleats and fuller sleeves are cute on your shape.

- Layer it up to add more dimensions to your shape.

- Any jeans and colors look good on you. Bleached and faded out effects on the behind and thighs give the illusion of curviness. Add a belt to low-rise jeans for extra hips.

Bypass: Baggy tops, tunics, and sweetheart neckline tops and dresses. Baggy clothing will not do anything for your shape.

Now, of course, you can choose to wear whatever you want no matter what shape you are, but the above tips give guidance on what will compliment you most.

Bras & Shapewear

Before shapewear comes into play, you want to make sure you're wearing the right size bra. I worked at Victoria's Secret as a bra specialist and realized that over 70% of women are wearing the wrong bra size and don't even know it. I believe I became the top bra salesperson during that time, because I wanted women to be comfortable in theirs with the correct fit, which unlimitedly would make them feel and look great.

Some smaller chested women want to look larger, and some larger chested women want to look smaller—I get that. You can get the look you want in the correct bra size. I also recommend getting a bra measurement minimally once a year. Go into a lingerie store that does bra measurements or conduct one on yourself.

Bra Self-Measuring Steps

1. Grab a flexible measuring tape and get started.
2. Use the side with the biggest number on it and use the tip as your guide.
3. Take the measuring tape across the back, under the under arms and bring it together from under the arms until it goes above the chest area.
4. Once you bring the measuring tape together to where it meets, look at the number the tip lands on. If it lands on an odd number round up. For example, if it lands on a 33, round it up to a 34.
5. Next, bring the measuring tape around your back, under your arms and across the widest part of your breast. As you're bringing the measuring tape together to where it meets, don't make it too tight. Leave just a little bit of room
6. Count big numbers going up to get your cup size. For example, if it lands on 35 and our first measurement from before was 34, we would count up to the number it lands on. If it landed on 34 it would be an A cup, 35 (B), 36 (C), 37 (D), 38 (DD), and 39(DDD). In this example, the first measurement of 34 and second measurement of 35 is a 34B.

 See my live example at **youtu.be/R58jKKL80gk**.

Depending on your shape, if, for example, you're a 34B you can also wear a 36A or 32C. If you aren't able to be 100% comfortable in your original measurement, you can try a custom fit by going up one number and down one cup size or down one in number and up one cup size.

Signs that you're wearing the wrong bra size:

- Breast spills out over the bra lining across your chest
- Constantly adjusting the positioning or straps
- Feels like it's digging into your skin
- More of your chest is out of the bra than it is inside
- You see deep bra prints on your body once you remove your bra

Having the right size bra on is worth your daily comfort.

Shapewear

Shapewear gives your body a natural enhancement. It smooth's out your clothing and gives you a slimmer look. Some women can even use it to give an added inches look.

Shapewear should give you some comfort vs. being in pain. If you're more uncomfortable than comfortable with everyday shapewear on, there is a problem. Know this: some shapewear is not meant to be worn all day, and some is everyday shapewear. Another thing that's good to know is the type of shapewear you need for a particular garment before you purchase it/wear it. Try it on first ladies, try it on. Shapewear is for your shape, it tucks you in, lifts you, slims you, and balances your look all at once. It's good to know which shapewear is for which body parts.

Take a look at the shapewear photo to see the variety of styles. They are to be worn correctly. Watch out for some of the shapers you have to step into, because they tend to show prints through your clothes. We should not see your shaper printing through your pants. Nor should it hang down past your skirt.

Some ask, "Do skinny/smaller built women need to wear shapers?" Typically no, but

MODEL BEHAVIOR: GET COACHED. GET BOOKED. **GET PAID.**

it still depends on the way they are proportioned.

Find the shapewear that is best for you. Shapers can help a pair of jeans that couldn't button now button and even smooth out a muffin top.

It's a great idea to spend time studying this so you will know which is best for you. Also, it is good if you can get both hair and clothing stylists that understand this.

Stats get the easy part done first. Know your bust, waist, and hips like you know your phone number. Wait, some don't know that with the new tech these days. So, like you know your address.

Guys have simple options to pull it together and ladies have many.

For some this may not be the case, but in most cases it is. Sometimes you will get a casting director that falls in love with someone's personality over image. In some

cases it will outweigh their image, and they can fix them up to be powerful through their personality.

As we all know, unfortunately, people judge you from your looks first—here is where the power comes in. Dress ready. Dress like a model who is serious about her business. Don't leave the house without wearing your confidence.

When your hair is a 10, makeup a 10, walk a 10, photo a 10, and overall look a 10— YOU GET TENS across the board.(flips hair)

Can't leave this stage without mentioning makeup. Makeup enhances your natural beauty when applied correctly.

I launched a lip collection back in 2012 and described it as awe inspiring, saturated, shimmering, protected, and plumped lip-gloss—lol. I wanted a product that would have all that in one to accommodate the variety of women. Signature Ink Cosmetic Collection is a makeup product that enhances natural beauty and provides a GLAM gloss line for kids and teens. More information and products will be available to you soon on **www.modelbehavior.life**

Skin

As a model, you will have to get very comfortable wearing makeup. An artist will apply your makeup for your print work, shows, etc. You're not going to be allowed to say "I don't wear makeup" and expect to be a part of the project or even get paid.

Problems come in when we aren't taking care of our skin after the makeup is on and/or are sharing eye/lip pencils and brushes that are not clean.

One of my bad habits I had to break years ago was sleeping in makeup and then waking in the morning and washing it off. That is such a no-no for your skin. I spoke with a Malika Tucker, Licensed Esthetician and Mua, and she really gave me the scoop on a good skin care regimen. Here is what she wanted you to know...

Skin Care Daily Regimen

Taking care of your skin is extremely important. Some of the most basic but key components to skin care are to keep the skin clean, moisturized, protected from the sun, and hydrated.

Morning Routine:

- ☐ Cleanse (use a cleanser best for your skin type)
- ☐ Tone (rebalances the PH of the skin)
- ☐ Moisturize (use an SPF of 30 or higher ALL year long)

Nighttime Routine:

- ☐ Cleanse (make your night time cleanse your deepest cleanse)
- ☐ Exfoliate (2–3 times per week). Your exfoliator can be a scrub or an enzyme type of exfoliate
- ☐ Mask (2–3 times per week on the same days you exfoliate)
- ☐ Tone
- ☐ Moisturize with a night cream (night creams are usually heavier, because they replenish the skin from the hard work it has done throughout the day)

WATER, WATER, WATER!!

Just like many things in life that need water to be sustained, so does our skin. Drinking plenty of water is not only great for our bodies in general but our skin, also. Our skin takes on a lot throughout the day. The benefits of drinking water as far as the skin is concerned are that it helps keep the skin clear and hydrated, removes toxins, and reduces the appearance of fine lines and wrinkles.

Basic Makeup Application:

Makeup is continually evolving and becoming more creative from glitters and jewels to vibrant lip colors. However, the simple look—the less in more look—is being more appreciated. The goal for makeup application is to enhance your natural beauty and your features and still look like yourself.

After following the above daytime routine, here are some basic makeup application steps:

- Concealer (use a concealer the same shade but no lighter than one shade of your natural skin color)
- Foundation (match your foundation along your jawline or neck for the most accurate color selection) you may need two foundation shades, one for spring/summer and the other for fall/winter.
- Brows (fill in brows with the color of your brow hair; DO NOT use black or colors darker than your hair)
- Eyeshadow (for daytime, use more natural tones like browns, taupe, bone, etc.)
- Mascara
- Eyeliner
- Blush or bronzer (be mindful of color choices not too bright or too illuminating)
- Lipstick/lip gloss
- Lip colors are fun, and you can be a little more explorative here depending on the occasion. Doing a natural face allows you to step out a little with the lips—just remember to still choose colors that are flattering on you.

Thanks, Malika, for sharing with the readers these quality steps.

Image becomes power after you accept THAT YOU ARE FEARFULLY AND WONDERFULLY MADE.

Image Challenge

What is your face shape? what is your body shape? What will you try now that you received more information about your shapes? Find one face, in real life or on television and match up with the face shapes on the chart. Continue to research your face/body shape and look and feel your best. If needed, speak with an image consultant, wardrobe stylist, or designer to meet your needs.

STAGE 11
you are the brand & the boss

It doesn't matter if you're an aspiring model or experienced model. Now is the time to treat modeling like a business and boss up. Get very serious about taking care of business. We live in a time now where you can be or become your own brand like never before. You can create your own destiny. People are becoming celebrities through Youtube views and videos going viral just by being themselves and using their talents and gifts to the best of their ability and not being afraid of standing in their own power—and you can do the same.

YOU ARE THE BRAND

Personal branding can be a lot of fun if you build your brand on everything you love and are passionate about pertaining to your career. Let your passion be the driving force for your brand.

Here are four ways you can start branding. Agency models, you will need to check with their agent and/or review your contract before doing this to make sure you don't breach it. You don't have time for that.

Choose your brand name

Yes, it can be your own name or a name that has a ring to it. Make it memorable, different, or something that stands out (in a good way). You can also use unique words for description like model, runway, male, curvy, etc. These keywords will help people find you, and it will help identify you. Some examples include @yourname, @yournamethemodel, @runwayyourname, or @curvymodelyourname.

Search your brand name on all social media channels to see if it's available. Facebook, Instagram, Twitter, Youtube, Snapchat, etc. Instagram should be like your informal online portfolio. Someone should be able to go to your profile and understand very clearly that you are a model.

If available, try your best to be consistent on all social media and domain names before starting the accounts. For example, you can find me @theedaniellebaker everywhere, and my domain is theedaniellebaker.com. Now, Twitter and a few others will allow only a certain number of characters. In this case still keep your brand name, just shorten it like I did. My brand name was too long for Twitter, so I shortened it to @theedanielleb.

Now with my newest brand Model Behavior, the website domain is www.modelbehavior.life. IG, FB @modelbehaviorlife & twitter @modelbehavior and in this case @modelbehaviors on snapchat because (modelbehaviorlife) was too long and (modelbehavior) was taken. As you can see sometimes that will happen, however keep it as close to exact as you can. Even if you're you not on majority social media at the moment still get them all as you're using the ones you're active on. That way if you decide to utilize them in the future it's already yours. Having a consistent name across the board will help tremendously with branding. If you currently have different handle names, you should be able to change them if the name you desire is available.

Check you're brand name on Go.daddy.com to see if it's available for a domain. Keep your website updated. If you don't have a website now, you will eventually want one as part of your business for branding and booking purposes. It's best to have an identifiable domain name. This is also your formal online portfolio. Add a testimonial page to your website. Clients love to see what other clients have said about working with you. So it's good to ask for feedback after your gigs. I would do it the same day or send an email back within 24 hours.

Also, be sure to have a booking form on your website for clients to book you. Having a booking form not only shows your level of professionalism, but it also will help you get the full details of what the client is booking you for.

If you do not have a website, you can still create a booking form that comes with a url link to your form. That way when someone wants to book you, you can send them the link to your form to fill out. Look online for some form building sites. I really like jotform.com, because its has templates, and it's really easy to use. Also, once you get your website, you will be able to embed your form on your website.

Your brand is your business—treat it as such. Only post things that will help you Get Booked & Get Paid, not hinder you.

Ask yourself, "If an agency, casting director, or client were interested in me, would they hire me after seeing this?" If the answer is no, don't post it. Just like regular jobs, where employers take a look on potential employees' social media as part of their interviewing/hiring process, so are the people in the modeling industry. Represent your brand the best you can. It's easy to destroy your reputation in the world today and in the industry. If agents think you're lazy, rude, unprofessional, or stuck on yourself, they don't want to be bothered. Trust me, they talk—the agents, photographers, designers, directors, and styling team all talk.

Social Media Etiquette & Hashtags

- Don't air out your dirty laundry or anyone else's on any public platform.

- Be careful what you're posting directly on your page and even commenting on others. If you're always negative or have bad things to say, clients may not want to work with you. To them, that's a first impression. Stay away from the potty mouth, too; it can turn off the fans you're building as well as the clients.

- Create your own hashtag with your handle name as well, and use it in addition to the other relevant hashtags. Repeat, hashtags like #model, #runwaymodel, #printmodel, #modelforhire, #modeling, #malemodel are all relevant.

- Starting your own hashtag is simply that. #_____—use this and you will see it begin to build. Sometimes it's a catch 22; because you created your own, whenever someone clicks or searches, only you will come up. On the other hand, hashtags like the ones above are saturated with models, but clients are going to those hashtags to find people to work with. Only use hashtags that connects with your branding. Not things like #bored.com or #Peoplearegettingonmynervestoday . What does any of that have to day with your brand? It doesnt.

Instagram tip: A marketer recently shared with me to put up to 30 relevant hashtags in the comment section after you post a picture on Instagram. Do not put all the hashtags in the description of the photo.

Engage with clients you desire to work with (casting directors, agencies, photographers, muas, hairstylists, fashion show producers, coaches, etc.).

Follow, like, and comment—these will keeps you engaged and also keep you in the loop with what they have going on.

Brand accounts should be PUBLIC
I can't tell you how many times models send potential clients to a private account. They don't have time to send you a request and then wait for you to accept. You can lose the opportunity right in that very moment. Make it easy for clients to view your work, and pique their interest. Also, follow the clients you want to work for, and stay in the loop of everything they have going on. Opportunities could be staring you right in the face.

Sexy Photos
Have you noticed by now that the sexier the photo it seems like the more likes or attention the photo gets? Skin is always in, but is that really where you want to be? Posting nudity, half naked photos and anything degrading yourself will hurt your brand. It will also attract the wrong attention, like predators and/or people that

have something totally different in mind. If you're a lingerie or vixen model, keep it respectful and tasteful.

Model Tip: Even when it comes to your private accounts, don't post pictures on the Internet you don't want to haunt you one day. It doesn't matter if it's in direct message/inbox or something you think is private. Although you can delete it once it's put on the Internet, understand that it will leave from where you deleted it, but it will not be completely erased from the Internet. You will think it has been deleted, and next thing you know it's in Google images.

Blogging

I personally feel that more models should blog, and I'm going to tell you why. When you're blogging about everything you're doing in the modeling industry, you're building content that people can see and learn more about you from. It's also like your digital time capsule, because your blogs will be archived, and you will always have them. You can go back and see how far you've come, all the memories, and more. You can build a blog as part of your website or just start with a blog.

Things to do if you already have these steps in place

- ☐ Go back through all your posts and ask yourself the question discussed above. If the answer is no, delete it.
- ☐ If your brand names are not consistent, change them to make them unified.
- ☐ It's okay to have multiple social handle names. Just make sure that the one you're using for your modeling business stays hirable.
- ☐ Be sure you match your brand.

Some think branding is all about logos and products; in this case it's not. Nor is it about keeping up with your competition and trying to do exactly what they're doing. Bring the uniqueness out about you and allow your biggest assets to be a part of that. Branding can take time—the longer you wait to get started, the longer it will take for you to create a buzz. It's never the perfect time to start branding, it will always be something going on or something to do. Just get to it right away.

Model marketing tools are your brand's best friend

When you have these marketing tools available, it helps enhance your brand from a magnifying class.

- ☐ Portfolio
- ☐ Comp cards
- ☐ Business cards
- ☐ Websites or social media pages for business
- ☐ Self-promotion (both freelance and agency models must promote themselves)

Following the steps above will help you begin to lay the foundation for yourself. Once you have these things in place, it's time to start creating a buzz about your brand. Start with your family and friends. Some of them will wholeheartedly support you, and some of them won't. This is not the time to get caught up in your feelings about it. I'm telling you now, it will become a distraction for you if you do.

You know your family and you know your friends, so you will know the best way to introduce your brand. Be serious about this; if it's all fun and games for you, they will not respect what you're doing. Then it becomes fun and games for them, too.

Choose to have a one-on-one talk with the people closest to you and/or have a family gathering or girls night out. You can make it formal or informal, depending on your group. Show them your photos, tell them about fashion events you've done, your goals, etc. Take a deep look at your list and see if any of them can be resources. You may have an uncle who does photography on the side or know someone who does. Your friend could be a good writer and can help you with your blog. You may have an aunt that does hair, etc. See if they believe in you enough to be a part of your team. And always leave the door open for financial help. If you need help, let them know what you need; you never know who might donate to/invest in your brand. However, you must have a plan.

Maybe you already have a support team/village of people to keep you encouraged and who believe in your brand and are supportive in the areas you need help the most. Great! You can still bring them together and discuss how far you've come and what your goals are now. You can give them handwritten thank you cards for all they have done for you so far. Or think of some ways that you can give back to them. On another note, with or without your family and friends' support, BOSS UP.

Boss Moves

Let your excuses RIP (rest in peace)
That's right—let them die. I would say put them to bed, but then you or someone else will end up waking them up again.

1. Write down 20 things you've been complaining about, and if that's not all of them, keep listing until you're done. Look back over the list of complaints and see all the things that have been holding you back from standing in your boss power.

2. Next time you want to get mad, get mad at everything you've been complaining about. Take that complaining list and burn it. As you're setting fire to the paper you're setting fire back in your life.

3. Then, count your blessings by writing down at least 20 things you're thankful for. Every time you want to complain, see the good and count a blessing. You will start to see your life change by creating a new normal.

Distraction Detox
Focus on your path and cut out people, places, and things that are a distraction for you.

1. Write down one to three people who you know are a distraction for you. This is both family and friends that you communicate with the most. People that are a distraction are negative people—their energy is negative, their talk it's negative, they absorb all your time, they drain you, and they keep you busy doing things that take you away from your focus. If they aren't adding to you, then they are taking away from you. If you have more than three people, write their name, too. How much longer will you let this negativity beat up on the good in you?

2. Do the same thing for places and things that are a distraction. If you're always on the Internet or the phone or going shopping or to the club, then these can be a distraction for you. What are you spending the most time doing that's not getting you any results? Time is not going to wait for you and neither are opportunities.

3. Once you've made your distraction list of people, places, and things, choose one of these words to write beside it to start your distraction detox. The goal here is to eliminate all of your distractions ASAP.

   - Immediate STOP (cut off, done, finished)
   - Conversation (discussing honestly what's best for you)
   - Slowly but surely day by day cut back on giving it attention until it's eliminated
   - Write it AWAY (every time you think about it, write down how you're feeling and cut or rip it up or burn it until you no longer think about it). There is a change when you physically do this.
   - Eliminate and replace (If it's a negative place, replace it with a positive place to spend time. If negative people, replace with spending time with positive people.) I know this can be hard, but it's even harder to continue to allow your to be in negative space.

Set Goals & Activate Them

1. Create a vision board with only the goals you're willing to work for.
2. Get yourself in an attitude of gratitude by writing down or saying all the things/people you're currently grateful for. Spend at least 10-15 minutes on this daily.
3. Look at your vision board daily and spend time visualizing your goals as if they're already reached.
4. Meditate when visualizing, feeling the feeling of having it now. You're living out your vision through your mind and whatever happens in the mind can become your reality.

5. Once your goals are beginning to be accomplished, add them to the back of your vision board or start a new board of all your accomplishments. Meditate in gratitude for the goals that have been reached.

The key to these steps is actually doing them, so you can activate your vision.

Handle Your Business

1. Be professional at all times, even when others are unprofessional. Be resilient when adversity comes.
2. Put yourself on a budget, reward yourself, pay yourself (MDI). Yes, Yes! Do what you say you're going to do.
3. Keep your commitments to yourself and stand in your truth.

Stop seeing competition, start seeing opportunity

1. Time is too valuable to waste on comparisons. You are your only competition. Compete with who you were last month, or even last year. When you compete with others, you get distracted. There is no way you can be creative and at your best if you're putting out competitive energy. Your mind will be occupied with junk, and next thing you know negativity will be getting dressed with you in the morning.
2. Don't let people control you and your emotions.

Always bring your slay game. Ha!

- Be bold, you're a boss.
- Make yourself proud.
- Try wanting to be like YOU when you grow up. The person you want to become in the next 15 years. Take your face shape and body shape and turn your image into power.

Stand In Your Truth

Don't go against your morals, standards, or something in your gut that you know isn't right for you to please someone else. Doing that eats away at your self-esteem and breaks you down slowly. You let people start controlling you unconsciously. You become weak and double-minded. You'll find yourself doing more and more things that are taking you further away from yourself. Let that fear go. Be true to yourself—the truth will always set you free. Even if it just brings you peace in your inner being.

Boss Up!

BOSS UP MODEL CHALLENGE

There is a boss in you wanting to give you boss thoughts, come out and speak for you, fight, and show up for you all the time.

Now I'm going to challenge you to BOSS UP. Get your Boss Book out and complete the boss moves below. You're either going be a boss and do these moves, or you're going to let someone else boss you around. Don't go to Stage 12 "Show Me the Money" until you can do these steps and "Show Up Like a Boss." Control your distractions.

MODEL BEHAVIOR: **GET COACHED.** GET BOOKED. GET PAID.

STAGE 12
show me the money

Models typically start off on a local level doing print ads, fashion shows, and promotions. People always ask how long before they can get paid. It can be your first job or your 20th job. No one can determine that on the day you say you want to model unless you're at a casting and they want to book you.

The thing is always being at your best; be ready, and stay ready. That means have your brand ready, your image ready, and all of your marketing tools. Go into casting at your best, and give them your best always. Make it hard for them to say no. If you're a freelance model and they don't have a budget, be so good they create one for you.

Ask, Believe, Receive your payment...............

Listen, some of you are not getting paid because you aren't asking for it. Don't be afraid to ask to be paid. Clients aren't afraid to ask you to participate, are they? It can be tricky when you're first starting out because you don't have experience yet, but if you have the look they're looking for, they might give you paid training.

Keep in mind that if you never done runway in a fashion show before and you ask to be paid, it may not be a yes. However, if you have the look they need for a shoot, they just might prepare you for that great shot. If you ask and they say no, don't get discouraged. You have just as much power to say no to jobs that you feel aren't a good fit for you as well. Agency models will need to discuss with their agent first.

Another thing that holds models back from getting paid is FEAR. I know it sounds strange, but believe it or not some feel they aren't good enough yet. Or they begin to put a timeframe on themselves instead of building confidence.

What's mind boggling for me are the models that have been in the industry for 5–10 years who say they have never got any form of payment in the modeling industry.

My questions to freelance models are, "Have you ever asked? Was your b.i.m. (Brand, image, marketing) at its best?"

My questions to agency models are, "Have you looked into finding another agency? Was your b.i.m. (brand, image, marketing) at its best?" Did you read your contract thoroughly? Can your agency be taking your money? Just like in the entertainment industry, artist experience music labels taking advantage of them for their lack of knowledge and reading contracts before signing…the same thing can happen with a modeling contract.

Models, don't do the same thing year after year after year if it's not working for you. That's insanity.

Now, let's say you get the gig that is paying and the client asks you your rate. Here is where freelance models can get stuck. This is not the time to say things like whatever you can give or it doesn't matter or ask what they normally pay. I need you to know your rates, hourly, flat rate (2–4 hours), and day rate (6 or more hours) at the bare minimum. Before you give a rate, know exactly what they are booking for. By this time you should have done some research or asked enough questions to get a full understanding. Use that booking form I was telling you about in the branding section. This way the client will fill out the form you created with all your questions in there.

Here are some questions you can use for your booking form:
- Name:
- Position:
- Company:
- Website:
- Email:
- Contact number:
- Date of booking:
- Type of booking: (you can add a drop down menu of the types of modeling you do or leave it for them to fill in)
- Hours needed:
- Location:
- Budget: (this is where they can put what the gig pays)
- Comment area (or ask for a description of the gig)

Some other options are:
- Referral (if someone referred you, go back and thank them)
- Company social media (this way if you aren't familiar with them, you can go to their pages to learn more)
- Once they submit this, you will receive a copy in your email/site. Having this form will already have given you an idea of what is being asked of you.

Believe

You have to believe in yourself, your brand, and what you can do. Your confidence level needs to be at an all-time high, but I don't mean cocky. If you don't believe in yourself, why should someone pay you?

One thing that gets my blood boiling is when models ask me do I think they have what it takes to be a successful model...and I come back with, DO YOU THINK YOU HAVE WHAT IT TAKES?? It shouldn't matter what I think about your dreams and the vision you have for your life. What matters is what you think.

Continue to do your MDI as we discussed previously in the model challenge. This will help boost your confidence tremendously.

Receive your payments…

What does Cuba Gooding Jr. say in that Jerry Maguire movie? "Show Me The Money."

Models get paid based on levels of tenure/experience and their look. Depending on the type of agency, you can receive bonuses and raises. Freelance models can receive hourly rates or flat rates. Depending on the flow of your modeling income, age, and state requirements, you will need to get familiar with 1099 and W9 forms for tax purposes.

We all like instant gratification, right? If you did a job, ideally you want to get paid directly afterwards. Or, if this was a 9–5, you'd want your check within two weeks. Here's the reality … The modeling industry doesn't work like that. There is some time in between on most jobs, especially those that come through an agency.

Here is an example if you're signed with an agency:
Agencies will give their models vouchers or a voucher book to take on jobs with them. The vouchers will already have all of the agency information listed, and the book will contain carbon copies—a copy for the agency, one for the client, and one for the model to keep in his/her records. Upon completion of the job, the client will fill out the voucher and sign it. As a model, you must sign it as well and take it back to your agency. Your agency will explain exactly how they want the vouchers filled out. Once your agency has received it, they will send the invoice to the client. From there the client will pay the invoice, normally through a check, but nowadays some complete online. Once the agency receives the payment, they will take out their commission and any other fees that the agency took care of and then pay the model. Realistically, it can be 30–90 days before you receive your money. However, if after 90 days the client hasn't paid for whatever reason, I'm sure your agency will be doing their best to track down the payment so that both of you can get paid.
If the client doesn't pay, then both the model nor the agency will get paid. So that should make you feel a little more comfortable knowing that agencies will fight for payments if it comes to that.

MODEL BEHAVIOR: GET COACHED. GET BOOKED. **GET PAID.**

Freelance models, you can also do this as well as a best practice for your business. Here is where model and entrepreneur meets and you become "modelpreneur." Brand + Boss = Modelpreneur. This is the winning combo.

You can find model voucher templates on the Internet or create your own. Put your brand name on them and personalize it the best way that will help keep you organized. Clients will give you that much more respect when they see you're about your business. Some jobs may be up for negotiation, but if you don't have anything to bring to the table, that's like negotiating for a new job and during the interview telling the manager you have no experience for the job but are asking for maximum pay. At that point you will either get minimum wage, or they will hire someone else for the job. Go for negotiation when you have built up your confidence and experience.

Even if you haven't started getting paid yet and you're building your brand, use your vouchers. Act like you're getting paid, fill out the voucher, and put the amount you felt you were worth getting paid. This will begin to put you in a state of attracting more jobs and actually getting paid for them. Also, you want to start practicing this so that when it really happens, you're ready. Lastly, filling it out will help you keep track of what you're doing pertaining to what you love. Those who are already getting paid can begin using vouchers to keep track for tax purposes.

Outside of monetary, payments can come in different forms for freelance models (especially new models). These particular ones can give you more of an instant gratification.

Travel expenses (meals, transportation, hotel stay)

- Giftcards
- Apparel
- Store credits
- Styling services
- Photo shoots
- Promotion (flyers, website, press release, radio, tv)

Always make it a win–win—a win for the client and a win for you. Just like I suggested that you post only things that will help you, only take jobs that will help you and not hinder you. If you're building your modeling experience and you really want to participate in something because YOU KNOW it's a win for you to be a part of, by all means, participate. However, don't do it just because. Find out if casting agents will be in the audience and if you need to network with someone or build a relationship with the producers. Remember, this is your brand, which means this is your business. There's nothing like being paid for doing what you love to do.

Here's the other side of getting paid. YOU MUST DELIVER. Don't hold back, let your BEST out. If you don't deliver, you better believe people are going to hear about it. Clients will be pissed off; they have stopped hiring models from certain agencies just because of one model. Think about it—wouldn't you be upset if you paid for something and didn't get what you thought you were going to get? Think about the last time your food or service wasn't right or even bought something and got it home and realized it wasn't worth what you paid. It's even worse for paying clients, so be ready to do your part.

Now, when you're at a job … it is NOT the time to discuss rates. It doesn't matter if this person is in the same agency as you or part of the team or not. Do not discuss any agreements already set nor change something outside of what your agency discussed with you. You don't want to mess up future bookings for yourself and/or someone else.

Even freelance models will be looked at unprofessionally in this situation. Once you make a deal with a client, show up and do your job. Don't arrive and try to persuade, complain, or negotiate something else. It UNPROFESSIONAL, and you will decrease your chance for future bookings.

What It Takes To Get Paid
For you as an aspiring model to be successful in the fashion industry, you need to be knowledgeable, have the look, be passionate, and maintain the perseverance needed.

Knowledge
Keep up with the latest models, designers, and photographers. Fashions and trends are good to know, too.

Do you know who's the highest paid model in the world and why? Do your research, I'm challenging you to find out. Then look to see what models are getting paid in your category of the modeling industry (e.g., supermodels, promotional, petite/commercial, curvy, male, children, etc.). Its questions like these you need to know the answer to. It's going to benefit you to know of the models getting paid and who's hiring them. And male models are getting just as much work as female models and sometimes out doing them quarterly.

Here's the thing, becoming knowledgeable brings you benefit, while lack of knowledge will do you great harm. If you're going to be in this industry, read and study.

For fashions and trends, subscribe to high fashion magazines like W Magazine, Vogue, GQ, Muse, Flaunt, etc. Also, learn more about fashion designers and their clothing lines. See what types of models they use that shows their designs well.

If you're unable to get magazines sent to your door, subscribe to their website and get emails. Follow them on social media and follow their blogs.

Attitude

Having the right attitude can take you a long way. Always stay professional no matter how big or small the job. Treat each assignment as though you are working for Vogue or the companies you have listed as your goals. The modeling industry is very close-knit, and word spreads fast, especially if you are a pleasure to work with. On the other hand, when the divas and divos come out in a negative way, the word spreads even faster. Negative attitudes will get you put on the blacklist. The blacklist is a list of models that clients DO NOT hire. They would rather work with models who display positive energy and attitudes as well as appreciation.

Show off in front of the camera and let the ego come out on stage, not on set when your suppose to be waiting patiently. Be grateful for every opportunity, introduce yourself, and say thank you to everyone involved in the job. And I mean everybody, from the hair stylist to someone who brings you water. SAY THANK YOU. Understand that no one has to do things for you. Anyone that can make things easier for you, save you time, and have strengths where you have weakness is worth some appreciation.

Confidence

Self-confidence is what sells to the clients. Designers want the message of their product emanated by someone who is confident. When meeting with a designer or casting agent, always maintains good posture and eye contact. Even though you have done all the right things and may get rejected, do not get discouraged and do not give up. You may not fit the profile of what they are looking for, but it doesn't mean you won't fit the next profile.

Discipline

Discipline is another key—you should be on time for everything. Being late sends the message to the designer and casting directors that you are a waste of their time. Time is precious in this industry and needs to be honored. There have been supermodels that have almost lost their contracts with major companies because of lack of discipline and poor decision-making. It takes a lot of discipline to make it in the modeling industry and even more to stay. Sometimes you have to sacrifice hanging out with friends, playing on the Internet without a focus, and spending money that you could have used toward investing in yourself and modeling career. Discipline is part of investing in yourself.

So now what? What are you going to do different? Will you read, research, and study? Will you get paid, go after what you really want, and be disciplined and make sacrifices? When are you going to activate your goals?

You hold in your hands a tool that will help guide and direct you if you let it.

NO EXCUSES.

If you have questions or any feedback, contact us: www.modelbehavior.life

If you're ready for model coaching with me: www.theedaniellebaker.com

You can live your dreams!

Dear Models,

Make your move—it's your turn. You don't have to wait to be discovered by someone else, you can discover you. It's your dreams that matter most and not what others have to say about you. Believe in yourself during the process. You see, many people never make it to their full potential because they give up during the process. But that's not you. You're going to go through a series of actions to reach your goals and live your dreams. Know that it's a journey of ups and downs with the beauty and the beast in this industry. One thing that is very important in your journey is believing and trusting in yourself. It's going to be that tug in your gut that wants you to do something that pushes you past your comfort zone, but your thoughts and emotions will want to fight you down until they knock you out… but KEEP MOVING. Take at least one step toward your dreams every day. That one step can be practicing, studying, researching, creating, casting, networking, or anything that will build toward your destiny. You will have to work for it, but YOU'RE WORTH IT!

I've been where many of you are right now. What changed for me was making a decision and staying committed to it. Often times, the things we struggle with are the things we haven't yet made a decision on. Decide what you want and move forward. When I was younger I came across a quote that became my favorite—even until this day. "Create your own experiences." You have the power to create your own experiences through your thoughts, actions, and the positive words you speak over your life.

I'm a fan of any of you who read this book and apply its principles. I care about what you do next. Make your move, because in making your move, YOU CAN MAKE IT!

Goodbye for now….

Your Favorite Model Coach,

Thee Danielle Baker

www.theedaniellebaker.com

CREDITS

AUTHOR
Thee Danielle Baker
www.theedaniellebaker.com

COVER MODELS
From Left to right
Nicole Kannon Wilmore
Freelance Model
IG: @_themodelkannon

Alex Bendit
Agency Model
Genesis Level Modeling Agency

Melanie Blankenship
Freelance Model
www.melanieblankenship.com

David Miller
Agency Model
In His Image Modeling Agency

Jearlean Taylor
Freelance Model
www.prettygirlblues.com

Christine House
Freelance Model
FB: @CEHMODEL

COVER PHOTO
Photography
Jazzy Studios

Hair By
Salon Chase
www.salonchase.com

Makeup By
Tyler Hale
beautitymebeat@yahoo.com

Idris Brown
stylesbyidris@gmail.com

SKIN CARE REGIMEN
Malika Tucker
Licensed Esthetician, MUA
Mtucker.le@me.com

PHOTOGRAPHY INSIDE BOOK
Signature Ink Photography
www.Signatureinkstudio.com

The Lab Baltimore
www.thelabbaltimore.com

Author Photos

Photography
www.thephotochase.com

Hair
@flyosophyluxe on IG

Makeup
Makeup By Tia
tannearab@gmail.com

ABOUT
Thee Danielle Baker

Thee Danielle Baker is a wife, mother, woman of faith and multi-passionate, award-winning entrepreneur. She loves helping those ready to demand attention visually and internally to produce results in their lives through fashion. To learn more about her and/or work with her, please visit her website at www.theedaniellebaker.com